THE
AMBIVALENT
DAUGHTER

MEMOIR *of a* CONFLICTED CAREGIVER

Bethanie Gorny

THE AMBIVALENT DAUGHTER:
MEMOIR of a CONFLICTED CAREGIVER
Copyright © 2023 by Bethanie Gorny. *All rights reserved.*

ISBN 978-1-66788-247-5 (Print)
ISBN 978-1-66788-248-2 (eBook)

AUTHOR'S NOTE:
The names of family members are their actual names. To respect the privacy of others mentioned in this book, the names have been changed. All the incidents and scenes described are true. Some of the dialogue may be slightly changed but to the best of memory using my journal as a reference, that is basically what was said.

In memory of my mother
Gertrude Fuchs Bauchner

Dedicated to
Merwin Fuchs and **Melanie Cutting**
who were unequivocal in
their devotion and support

*In recognition and appreciation of
caregivers everywhere.*

Contents

Preface

When my mother was eighty-four, she had a stroke that made her dependent on others for all her daily living needs, self-care, and medical care. From that moment on, everything in my life changed. I became the primary person in charge of her care and her finances. After a short time in a rehab facility, her doctors recommended that she be moved to a residential setting. My mother did not qualify for Assisted Living because she was not independent enough. The next level of care is a nursing home which is a residential setting with more care for people who are significantly disabled and require round-the-clock care and medical oversight. I wanted her near me and my choices were limited in southern New Jersey where I lived. To complicate matters, we had never gotten along. Our relationship was characterized by constant disagreements and fighting as well as distrust and resentment. But there was always an underlying current of love and devotion that revealed itself in climactic moments. The stroke, which changed both our lives dramatically, was one of those times.

Most memoirs on this topic feature a parent and an adult child with a loving relationship where the child takes on the role of caregiver with no misgivings, or an adult child who hates their parent and wants no responsibility for them or as little as possible. Few, if any, are about children with ambivalent feelings towards their parent, probably a more common scenario. They are neither martyrs nor spiteful, heartless children. I wanted to write an honest book about a caregiver who had conflicted feelings about her mother. I wanted to share the highs and the lows of the experience with others who are caregivers or will be. I approached my mother's care with ambivalence but also with confidence that I could oversee it. It was much harder than I imagined it would be, and although I did manage it, it was a daunting experience. Being the primary person responsible for my mother was an emotional roller coaster and my feelings ranged from overwhelmed, to depressed, to resentful, to epiphanies about our relationship, to joy, frustration, anger, and ineffable sadness. It's not an exaggeration to say that I am forever changed by the experience. I learned so much about myself and my mother. She was a physically active, very social woman who enjoyed her life immensely. Then, abruptly, all that was taken away from her. She reacted angrily when it was clear she was not improving. Later she became depressed. I'll never stop feeling sorry that her life ended that way, but I am grateful I was able to help as much as I could.

I began writing in a journal as an outlet for my feelings. I didn't write every day, but the journal served its purpose and recorded my experiences. It was there for me to review and gain perspective or see solutions to the problems that arose. This book is based on that journal. Everything in it is true. The dialogue is based on my recollection of those conversations supplemented by my journal. My mother was in two different nursing homes during the two years before she died. Two years is the average life span for people in nursing homes. For the sake of creating a reading experience that would not be redundant, I compressed those two years into one. The events described took place from 2003 to 2005 and yet they are as relevant today as they were when I wrote about them in my journal.

It took me years to decide to write about my caregiving experience, but I felt compelled to do it because I think others in my situation will learn that the feelings they are experiencing are normal and common. In addition, after doing research on nursing home problems today, I found they are much the same as they were when my mother and I were dealing with her care. Yes, some nursing homes have adopted new philosophies about nursing home care, like deinstitutionalization and making care more person centered, but most nursing homes remain traditional and the same problems I encountered exist today. I hope this book can be a guide to what a nursing home can be and what to look for when considering nursing home placement.

I never knew anything about the conditions in nursing homes until my mother was in one. What I found was that they emphasize medical care over human care. There are private nursing homes which are termed for-profit. There are also non-profit ones which are either publicly funded or charitable. The majority of nursing homes in the United States are private and want to make a profit for their investors. Whenever there is a profit motive in a human service, there is the temptation to make cuts that will build profits. During Covid I was not surprised to read about deaths in nursing homes that could have been avoided with more stringent laws covering nursing home operation. I wrote this book partly to call attention to the continuing problems and the critical need for nursing home reform. Only about 20% of aging adults spend their later years in nursing homes. The rest are taken care of at home, or in an assisted living type of residence. Those who are in nursing homes are generally too disabled to be in other types of care. My mother was such a person.

My memoir is for everybody who has cared for an elderly parent or will care for one. You may not have a parent who needs to be in a residential setting, but if you become a caregiver to your parent, you will experience momentous changes and revelations in your relationship with that parent. No matter how painful and difficult that time in your life is, if you accept the role of caregiver for your parent, it will also be an experience you won't regret. It may well be the first time you come to know your parent and yourself. It was for me.

CHAPTER 1

The Big Bang

September

It was the kind of brisk, sunny day that makes you feel an irresistible urge to be outside. I always thought of it as suede jacket weather, the time you got out that cool weather jacket, marking the transition between summer and fall. A breeze rustled through the trees and sent more leaves fluttering to the ground. It was a Friday, my day off from the college where I taught, so I didn't need to resist the pull of the outdoors. I put on my workout clothes and began my walk around the neighborhood. The musty smell of fallen leaves brought back memories of the huge piles of leaves my sister and I used to rake together on my grandmother's lawn for the sole purpose of jumping in them and throwing clumps of dead leaves at each other. Autumn is my favorite time of year; it always feels fresh and invigorating, like new beginnings. As a child and then as an educator, it was always September, not January, that signaled the start of a new year. I walked along the quiet streets thinking, what a perfect day! The day turned out to be far from perfect; a new beginning, yes, but not one I ever would have predicted and certainly did not wish for.

My phone rang just as I returned to the house. It was my sister, Melanie.

"Mom's had a stroke," she said, without preamble.

I gasped. "Oh no, how bad?"

"I don't know. She's in intensive care now."

Melanie didn't add much more, and I think that was all she could get out at the time. Then again, she's always been a person of few words. I told her I'd be right there. I packed an overnight bag, called my husband, Jack, at work, and jumped in my car. My big sister reflexes kicked in immediately. Melanie is only sixteen months younger, but we still held the traditional roles of big and little sister all our lives. As the big sister, I wanted to relieve her of some of the responsibility.

I sped up the Garden State Parkway from Atlantic City to the hospital in Elizabeth, New Jersey in record time, all the while thinking, but Mom is so healthy! Gertrude was eighty-four and in very good shape. She swam laps, bowled, did her own cleaning, and was completely independent. Her five foot three taut body was full of energy and strength. Her natural auburn hair, only slightly tinged with grey, was like a reflection of her personality, vivid and lively. She lived in her Florida condo but drove up to Elizabeth, New Jersey every spring and rented an apartment to escape the Florida heat and visit family and friends. She used to drive up with Ben, my stepfather, but when he died, she continued making the trip solo. That was when she was in her seventies and continued right up to this day. She always stopped overnight somewhere in the Carolinas arriving at my house the next day in time for lunch. Mom was legendary among all my friends (none of whom would have made such a trip alone) and anyone else who knew her.

As the monotonous Garden State Parkway scenery of green grass and highway lanes flew by for two hours, I focused completely on getting there. I didn't turn on the radio and didn't stop at the rest stop. I just kept driving with one thought in my head — I must get there quickly before something dreadful happens. I had a premonition that nothing would be the same from then on. Our relationship was always difficult, and I felt ambivalent about her much of the time, but I still felt love for her and I didn't want to lose her. Whenever the chips were down, I always wound up calling her to talk. Who would I call if she died?

As soon as I got to the hospital, I began trying to find out what had happened to my mother and what her prognosis was. I was immediately entangled in the hospital bureaucratic red tape: unable to talk to her doctor, unable to get much information, and besieged by requests to fill out paperwork and more paperwork. Meanwhile, Mom was unconscious and hooked up to an immense number of machines in intensive care. I stood outside the Intensive Care room with Melanie, staring through the glass at our mother. We were not allowed in. Mom's eyes were closed but her facial expression shifted back and forth from one of anguish to bewilderment, like she was in pain and couldn't figure out what was going on. The nurse assured me she wasn't in pain because she was highly medicated. If she could have spoken, Mom probably would have said, "What the hell happened?"

What happened was an aneurism exploded in the center of my mother's brain, and, like a volcano, spewed blood throughout both hemispheres destroying neurons in its path indiscriminately. It happened at, of all places, Newark Airport, a huge, busy, and confusing airport. My sister had arranged for Mom to pick her up when she flew in from Canada. Afterwards they were going to drive back to Mom's summer headquarters in Elizabeth and head off the next day for a family gathering at a mountain resort in New York.

Mom was indeed waiting at the gate as promised when my sister came through it, and she greeted Melanie effusively. Mom said she had to use the restroom before they left. She never came back out. Melanie went in to check on her and found her in an unlocked stall seated on a toilet unable to stand up. She helped pull Mom's pants up. Then she tried to help her walk out of the restroom, but it was clear Mom was experiencing great difficulty trying to walk. A bystander hurried over to a security guard and explained that there was a medical emergency.

Within minutes both the police and ambulance technicians arrived and strapped Mom onto a gurney. Melanie said Mom was calm although she seemed somewhat dazed, but she was not upset. As she was loaded into the ambulance, Melanie suddenly remembered that Mom had parked her car somewhere in the vast Newark Airport parking lot. She stopped the ambulance from taking off and asked Mom if she remembered where she had parked the car. Mom thought briefly and responded in slurred speech, "Oh, the end of one of the aisles." Her car keys were not in her purse and Melanie knew they were either lost or still in the car.

A police squad car drove Melanie around the indoor parking area. Miraculously, it took only a few minutes to locate Mom's car, door half open, keys in the ignition, engine idling for the last hour. Incredibly it had not been stolen. Obviously, Mom was not well when she drove to the airport and certainly not when she parked the car. The stroke must have been gathering steam by then, but nothing like a few little stroke symptoms would ever stop my stubborn mother from carrying out her intentions.

My sister and I left the hospital and drove to Mom's apartment. We spent the evening catching up on things and watching TV. It was an awkward situation because we hadn't been involved in each other's lives much over the past several years. Geography played a role, but we had been emotionally distant for years. The rift between us grew over the years beginning when we were children. I admit, I wasn't the best big sister and if I were her, I wouldn't like me either. A combination of sibling rivalry and a dysfunctional family caused many of our problems. Sitting on the sofa, watching TV, I felt the tension between us like a thick wall of ice that couldn't be chipped away although, as an adult, I regretted how far apart we had grown. I had tried to break through the barrier and develop a better relationship several times to no avail. Once I asked her why she never talked to me about her feelings, hoping she would start. She answered, "I don't do that with anybody. I don't feel the need to." And that was the last time I attempted to reconcile.

Now here we were, faced with a crisis that we had to confront together.

CHAPTER 2.

A Hurried Plan of Action

September, next day

I arrived at the hospital at seven AM and finally met the doctor and spoke to him. He explained the type of stroke Mom had had was profuse and could affect many functions of the brain. He thought her speech would be impaired, there might be cognitive issues, and there was paralysis on her right side. A lot of damage had occurred from the time of the stroke up to the time she was treated, the slim Asian doctor explained. The rest would unfold in the next few days and weeks he added, and then hurried away to complete his rounds.

I went back to Mom's room and met Melanie outside the ICU. We observed Mom through the glass partition as though she was some kind of new exhibit in a large aquarium tank. Her eyes were closed and she appeared to be grimacing and trying to move her head. Thinking she might be uncomfortable; I entered her inner sanctum and pushed the electric control button to adjust the slant of the bed to a more comfortable position. That bed had more positions than the Kama Sutra and was extremely quick. I tried to adjust the top half and soon had Mom going up and down like a lever almost uncontrollably. Miraculously, Mom didn't wake up. I looked over at my sister standing outside and we both started laughing. Soon we were giggling uncontrollably to the point of tears. I rarely ever had giggling fits except when I was with my sister. It felt like old times when we were young and spent a lot of time together. I welcomed that moment of connection and hoped it paved the way for more camaraderie going forward.

Standing in the hallway, we were still half laughing and half crying and then just crying. It was a moment of much needed emotional release. I explained what the doctor had told me.

"Well, maybe he's wrong," said Mel.

"Maybe," I agreed, but I was not as optimistic as my sister. I was trying to placate her and not dash her hopes. We had to get along. I knew we had to put aside our differences and focus on Mom and doing what was best for her. The strained relationship I had with my sister was partially the result of the nature of my relationship with Mom and partially due to being a somewhat overbearing, critical older sister. Mom and I fought and argued continually over the years, while Melanie loved her unconditionally and got along well with her. They were close in a way I envied — their roles were still the same as they were long ago — a protective mother and her beloved younger child. It was always obvious that Mom favored her — she was an easier child to raise. Now all three of us would be together trying to cope with whatever came next in Mom's life. We were a triangle, and all the angles were dependent on each other.

The next day my Uncle Merwin arrived around noon with his son, Phil. Merwin, Mom's only sibling, was the most important person in her life besides my sister and me. He was twelve years younger, but the age gap never stopped them from having a close relationship. He and my mother had no other siblings. It was comforting to see him, and I was happy to have another voice in the matter besides

Melanie. I remember how my mother talked about him with such love, her baby brother, how she always looked forward to being with him. All the old photos record their relationship as being a close one. I can recall a picture of my twelve-year-old mother pushing baby Merwin in his carriage. I imagine she took care of him almost like a second mother as he was growing up. I remember how Merwin always called her Gertie and how he used to kid around with her. The affection between them was obvious, but not in a physically demonstrative way, because neither of them were. An exchange of smiles conveyed as much warmth as a hug between these two, but there were some hugs and kisses as well. Throughout their lives, they were always there for each other whenever times were difficult. I knew she would be glad to see him, but she was still too heavily medicated to respond to him.

Mom had been hospitalized for two days at this point and the hospital informed us it was time for her to transition to a rehabilitation center. Mom was able to speak with a little slurring, but we could understand her. Her right side was more affected by the stroke, and she couldn't move her arm and could barely move her leg. She was able to use her left arm, but not her left leg. Her cognitive skills seemed to be intact. Her condition had deteriorated rapidly from the time she met my sister in the airport. They say if you can get a stroke victim to the hospital in an hour, much of the damage can be minimized. My mother was in a hospital within an hour of the time she found herself unable to walk out of the bathroom in the airport and yet she was severely affected by the stroke.

Our little family met in the hallway outside my mother's room. We all agreed it was best if she continued her care near me since Canada is far away and complicated. Melanie needed to return to her family and her job and promised to make the eighteen-hour round trip drive to visit once a month. My uncle promised to make the three-hour round trip from his home in north Jersey to Atlantic City as often as he could.

What we didn't discuss was the fact that Mom and I never got along. She was headstrong and so was I. Melanie approached things differently. She was calm, nonconfrontational, and engaged in passive resistance to have things her way. It was ironic that I would be the sibling who would take on the most responsibility for my mother during this period of her life. I knew she would much rather have had Melanie, her favorite, be the designee, but it was not feasible. Although Mel offered, the problem of coordinating Canadian and American Medicare and American insurance would impact Mom's care in ways we couldn't foresee, so we all felt this was the best option.

All my life, I felt a continual sense of dread that a fight was about to erupt any time Mom and I didn't agree completely on something, which was often, yet I couldn't avoid every issue that we disagreed on. There were no calm discussions with Mom. If I didn't agree with her, she'd starting yelling at me. There was no in-between, no negotiation. By the time I was in junior high, we were fighting constantly, not necessarily about anything of consequence; it could be anything and everything. Whatever I wanted to do; she was against. Whatever I wanted; she saw no reason to have. Sometimes it seemed that she was oppositional just because it was something I requested. Her argumentativeness wasn't limited to me. She argued with her friends (they joked about it and said "if you say black, Gert will say white"), her husband, her mother. There was a lot of anger in our house, and I didn't understand it, but, as a child, I felt powerless to improve the situation. I was a rebellious teen and there was lots to rebel about in our home. I got married young in the last year of college to get away from home, but I didn't realize it at the time.

Going forward, I believed the problems between Mom and me would be minimal, given her weakened condition. How could she object to the decisions made when we all had had input, all had agreed? Surely, she would understand that this needed to be done and we were all trying to take the best care of her possible. It was all we could think of on short notice. None of us knew how long she would be in the rehab center, and we were planning only for a limited period.

And so I joined the ranks of the fifty-two million Americans taking care of elderly or disabled relatives. I was typical in that eighty-one percent of them are women. Like most thrust into this role, I didn't know what I was getting into as far as costs, placements, insurance, and all those basic things you need to know as a caregiver. I didn't know that forty-three percent of caregivers report the situation causes disputes among family members. And I didn't know about the emotional toll caregiving can take on the caregiver, the care recipient, and other members of the family.

I felt calm, mature, responsible; like I usually did in crises or in any demanding situation. I knew everything was falling on me, but it was the kind of thing I did well. I was often in a leadership role in my career. As a school administrator, I had grown used to managing problems successfully and I believed that I would be able to handle anything that came my way. After all, my role model was my mother, a strong, competent woman, who never seemed overwhelmed by anything. She chose her direction and headed for it like a guided missile. This new challenge was one I thought we would both meet with our usual take-charge aplomb. It had always worked in the past.

CHAPTER 3.

The Rehab Center /
Nursing Home Connection

Mid-September

The hospital in Elizabeth arranged for an ambulance to drive Mom to south Jersey to a rehabilitation center about twenty minutes from my house. By that time, Mom was talking and making sense. The spontaneous recovery associated with strokes in the first three months was taking place. Her mood was positive, although her right side was partially paralyzed. We all believed this would be a temporary situation based on similar cases the doctor shared with us.

Over the next few weeks, the rehabilitation center staff gave her every kind of therapy they could to improve her functioning. Whenever I visited, Mom was upbeat and optimistic about her therapies. They kept her remarkably busy with a daily schedule of speech therapy, occupational therapy, and physical therapy. Improvement in speech was steady and her cognition seemed normal, but the physical capabilities were moving along very slowly. I was beginning to worry that her current physical state would not improve.

When the Medicare money for rehabilitative services ran out, the medical team met and decided she needed an interim placement where she could continue to receive intensive therapy and complete care. We moved her to Pleasant Gardens, billed as a senior living center, and she was admitted to the rehabilitation section of their facility. A primary consideration was that it was only twenty minutes from my house so I could visit often. Medicare will pay for twenty days of this type of care. After that, another placement would be necessary.

I hoped it would be her condo in Florida, as did she. She missed her friends and her pleasant lifestyle down there. It had been twenty years since she and Ben, my stepfather, retired and moved down there, following a group of their closest friends. They all lived in a modest condo community and spent every day doing things together, from swimming in the pool, to playing mahjong and cards, to eating out at the many early bird specials. Sadly, Ben died only five years after the move. Mom missed him terribly and was grieving for over a year. She began volunteering at the library and maintained her social life with her friends who included her in their lives as they always had. She reached out to friends who had also lost their husbands. Jack and I took her on a family vacation with our kids to Jamaica a few months after Ben died and I think it was a welcome respite for her from the sudden loneliness she was experiencing. Eventually Mom began to enjoy her Florida lifestyle again. When the stroke occurred, she had been living on her own for the past seventeen years. Florida was her home now and as she put it, "My blood has thinned out down there and I can no longer stand the cold so there's no chance I'm moving anywhere else."

Mom was always such a determined person that I was sure she would overcome even this major setback. She could easily win the Most Stubborn Person award if there were one. And she was courageous. When World War II broke out, she enlisted and went to

Europe to serve her country despite her parents' strenuous objections. When she put her mind to something, little could deter her. I felt certain her strong will and courage would see her through this turn of events.

CHAPTER 4.

My New Life

October

While my mother spent her days on a strict schedule of therapies, I spent mine figuring out her finances. I had added a new facet to my life — taking care of my mother's life. At times it seemed like the new responsibilities were taking over my life. I went through all her papers, a monumental task. I began paying her bills, managing her insurance, trying to keep track of her medications, paying her co-pays, managing her banking, her Medicare, her Supplemental medical insurance, and conferring with her doctors and therapists. There were also pension payments and investments to keep track of. Luckily, she had given me power of attorney one year ago. It was her idea and one of the few times she was willing to acknowledge her mortality.

I tried to keep up with the friends and relatives calling or e-mailing to find out how "Gertie" was doing. I soon learned they didn't want to listen to the terrible details and would go silent on the other end of the phone. No one wanted to hear that she was in diapers and couldn't eat unassisted. I had to be honest and tell them she was paralyzed on one side and confined to a wheelchair, but I kept the details of how much her life had been diminished to a minimum and gave them what positive information I could. They were all around her age and I believe it depressed them to think this could be their fate someday as well. For some of them, it already was a reality as the health problems began to pile up. After a few months, most of them stopped inquiring. I believe it wasn't that they weren't good friends, because they were; most for many years, but they could just stand so much sad news. Still I was surprised that none had called to talk to her. They sent cards and notes and talked to me. A couple of them told me that there had been a few times when Mom seemed to zone out in mid conversation for a few seconds staring straight ahead and then would come back to the present. Or other times she got names and words mixed up. They didn't want to embarrass her and just let these incidents slide by. I now know that these lapses can be a precursor to strokes. I wish one of them had let me know this was happening. Maybe she could have gotten medical treatment that would have prevented the severe stroke she had.

As time went on, I felt like I was drowning in new, unfamiliar, time consuming responsibilities. My work as an assistant professor of special education four days a week took a lot of time, and now with the additional responsibility of being the primary person in charge of my mother's care, there was not a lot of energy left over for my husband. Jack was understanding and supportive, but he could do little to help me with my new duties. My mother had some assets, and I knew I needed to guard them carefully, so they would last until she got better. Unfortunately, there was no way to predict when that would be.

CHAPTER 5.

Some Things Never Change

There was tension between us even though I tried not to let it get in the way of her care and the ongoing decisions that had to be made. That's always the way it was with us. She wasn't easy to get along with, but neither was I. Our history was a tumultuous one. As a young child I was shy and withdrawn to the point where my teachers asked if something was wrong at home. What was wrong was that I was being brought up by my grandmother, a mean woman who was totally unaffectionate and hostile to Melanie and me.

Mom was at work five days a week and too tired to be very involved. Like her mother, Mom was not a very affectionate person. I noticed that the atmosphere was different in my friends' homes — there was a surfeit of physical affection and attention from both parents who seemed very involved in all aspects of their children's lives. I envied those children.

Mom believed in slapping and I can still remember the red handprints on my back or arms, never the face. She would just let loose in a furious torrent of slaps that landed wherever she could reach me as I struggled to get away. Once I ran out the back door and she ran right after me around the whole house until I was cornered and she could get to me and smack me hard several times. My grandmother was also a slapper and probably brought my mother up that way. Melanie got the same treatment, but she didn't get blamed as much for infractions. I was the more likely one to be slapped because I was the instigator and Mom knew it. I was the one who had the brilliant ideas and Melanie followed along.

While I was growing up, I actually didn't think it was a bad way to parent and I assumed that was how all parents dealt with their children. But physical punishment is remembered as a time when a parent becomes consumed by their temper and you see the parent as a different person, one who can suddenly change and let their temper take control. It didn't stop until I was around eleven or so when, as she raised her hand to hit me, I raised mine and said, "if you hit me, I'll hit you right back." She was shocked, but the slapping stopped that day.

We rarely got punished, but once in a while, Mom would take away privileges. For me, the worst punishment was taking away my books. The two tier shelf in the bedroom I shared with Melanie, filled with Little Golden books and beloved children's classics would suddenly be empty. I'd lie on the floor next to the shelf and cry to no avail. She put them back when she decided it was time.

As I got older, I began to assert myself and fought Mom every step of the way to be allowed to do what my peers did. I wanted permission to shave my legs, permission to ride on a public bus, money to buy little things for myself like a lipstick or a new sweater, permission to date, to stay out as late as my friends, and so on. The restrictions she placed on me had a negative impact on my social life. For example, it was a big deal to go with a girlfriend and take the bus downtown to shop. I wasn't allowed. Mom wanted to pick out all my clothes herself. She would take us shopping and pick out everything. Or she would go shopping alone and bring home clothes for me that she chose. For a long time, she dressed us alike. It was fine when we were little, but later on I wanted to be treated as an individual and I rebelled against that practice, too.

I recall the night of one of the first dances I ever went to in junior high and how allowing Mom to pick out my dress for that occasion resulted in total mortification. I wanted to buy a dress from a better store, but Mom insisted I get one from her friend who sold clothes out of her den. I arrived at the dance in a pea-green shirt-waist Mom said was just right for the occasion. Actually, it was suitable for a ladies luncheon. All around me, girls were wearing frothy pastel dresses fluffed up by numerous crinolines. I looked like a stalk of asparagus amid a bouquet of beautiful flowers. No one asked me to dance. In tears, I called Mom to pick me up. It was the last time I let her pick out my clothes. I began working in a department store on weekends to get a clothing discount and began purchasing much of my own wardrobe.

When I was thirteen or so, preteens were all starting to have their own phones with private lines. Spending time talking on the phone was like texting today. We all could spend hours talking to each other and making our social plans. Mom would get angry when I tied up the phone so much of the time, but still would not yield. I reasoned with her that if I had a phone with a private line like all my friends had she wouldn't have to deal with me being on the phone so much. Finally she relented and got one for Melanie and me to share. That pink Princess phone was my link to the social world I found myself in.

I worked as a babysitter, a cashier, or a waitress all through my high school and college years and supplied my own spending money. I was living a life that felt deprived compared to my suburban peers. I never got the impression that my mother refused to allow me privileges my peers had for moral or even financial reasons. I think she just didn't want to be inconvenienced by giving me some of the freedoms and choices I clamored for. It made her life more complicated.

She demonstrated little interest in me on any level. No matter what I achieved, she never complimented me. She never told me I was pretty, or smart, or talented in any way. I got good grades, played the piano well, got parts in school plays, and wrote little stories beginning in second grade. She seemed uninterested in me and I felt that she didn't like me, let alone love me. When it came time to apply to college, she never talked to me about it except to encourage me to go to a commuter college nearby and get a degree in education. I didn't think my parents could afford to send me away. I had dreams of studying literature and history and all the liberal arts, but that was not what I got in the teacher's college. Teaching turned out to be something I loved, though. For years, I put aside my writing dreams while I climbed the ladder of success in the education world eventually attaining my master's degree and then a doctorate.

Despite the fact that Mom and I never got along, if ever one of us was in trouble, the other one was right there for her, standing beside her, seeing it through until the problem was solved, or the crisis averted. We felt the pull of family ties in difficult times and rallied round each other. She loved to tell the story of how when I was about eight, a cop pulled her over for speeding and began speaking rudely to her. I leaned toward him from the back seat and said angrily, "Stop talking to my mother that way!" And he did.

I remember two times in particular when she went to bat for me. Once when I was in seventh grade. She knew that being part of a social group was important to me. I had been working to get accepted by a large group of seventh grade girls that were "in" and was making real progress when the most popular one invited the group to a pajama party at her house. She didn't include me. She was only slightly aware of me since I was new in the group. I was devastated and Mom knew something was wrong. She asked me and I told her. She took matters into her own hands, and, without my knowing, she called the girl's mother and explained how left out I felt and asked if her daughter would please invite me. She didn't know the woman and it took a lot of nerve on her part. The girl called me that night and invited me to her party. It was the beginning of a recognition on the part of that group of girls that I was a bona fide member of the group. Life in junior high and high school was easier for me from then on.

The other time that stands out in my memory was when my high school math teacher made me stay for detention because I didn't do my homework. I was the only one staying for detention with him that afternoon. After about twenty minutes, he offered to drive me home. I didn't think anything of it. He was a balding middle-aged man and I thought he was just being nice. Maybe he was. When he dropped me off, Mom saw his car and watched me get out. She asked who it was, and I told her it was my math teacher. I heard her call the principal and angrily tell her that she never wanted to have that teacher or any other drive me home and that it was completely inappropriate. And furthermore, she didn't want me coming home late, so keeping me in detention was unacceptable. She didn't want me walking home all alone at a late hour. Mom was protecting me from a threat I had no idea existed. I never thought a man that age would have any interest in me. But Mom wasn't waiting for anything to happen. She didn't get involved in my life often, but when she did, she was like a strong wind that could blow away the problem by whatever means she felt necessary.

Now, with the nursing home placement and her devastating physical condition, I knew this was one of those times when I had to be her advocate and come to her rescue because she was in big trouble.

CHAPTER 6.

Pleasant Gardens Rehab Center

October

On Wednesdays, I taught classes in the afternoon, so it was convenient to visit Mom in the morning and observe her in the rehab room. There are three sections in Pleasant Gardens: the nursing home section upstairs which comprises the largest portion of the building, the Alzheimer's unit, and the small rehabilitation section where Mom was living. It's a temporary setting for people who have recently been hospitalized and need full time nursing care while they receive therapies. Medicare will pay for eighty days of this type of care termed sub-acute. The patients either respond to therapy positively or they are moved to another type of residential setting. For some that was the nursing home floors upstairs. If a person was independent enough to be able to live in an assisted living setting, they were relocated to one of the many private facilities that provide that type of care which is not Medicaid eligible. Others are able to live with family or with home help. I was still hoping that Mom would get better and go back to her beloved Florida condo, maybe with a home care aide to assist her.

The therapists strove mightily to get damaged people back in shape. I would sit as unobtrusively as possible in a corner and watch them put my mother through her paces. They implemented strengthening exercises, coordination exercises, and some for simple stimulation. Mom tried valiantly to accomplish every task they set for her, but her legs just wouldn't cooperate. She was not close to walking. It was hard to see my active mother in a wheelchair. I cheered her on like a soccer mom and I believed that somehow my being there, encouraging her, would keep her focused and motivated.

Todd usually worked with Mom. He was a big, friendly guy with biceps like cannonballs and no neck. He put all that upper body strength to good use lifting and hauling people around the therapy room, supporting their weight as they tried to stand or walk. Todd pushed Mom to try her hardest just like an expensive personal trainer would. Mom enjoyed her sessions with him and believed he would get her walking again. I could tell Todd liked her and why wouldn't he? She was one of the few residents who had normal cognition and she was feisty; a pleasant change for him. She liked to kid around with him, too. I thought she was flirting a little. One day, as I watched Todd teach her how to lift weights with her arms and legs, Mom asked him if she was ready for the Mrs. America contest yet. "Not quite," he laughed, "but when I'm done with you, you'll be a contender." He stood directly in front of her, holding her arms to get her to take baby steps. It looked a little like they were dancing. Mom told him "you're a good dancer and this is a pretty good date. You're not Fred Astaire, but you'll do." "But Ginger, I'm having trouble keeping up with you," he quipped winking at me.

The forty-five-minute session always went by quickly. After therapy, I often stayed with Mom to keep her company during lunch. The patients in the rehabilitation section of Pleasant Gardens all eat together in a small dining room. Each table was set with a little vase of flowers. Tasteful unobtrusive music played softly in the background.

The walls were a dark evergreen color, and the chairs were uphol-stered in a cranberry and green flowered fabric that matched the window treatments. The whole room had the feel of a restaurant in an inn — slightly colonial, sedate, intimate. It was a pleasant place to have a meal.

The first time she ate there, Mom glared at her lunch and said, "This crap looks like someone already chewed it and spit it out." She was accurate in her description. Her swallowing capability was weakened by the stroke, so her diet consisted of pureed food because of the danger of choking. I assured her that gradually she would get food with more texture, but it was too soon. Mom had not learned to use her left hand that well, but she was getting a little better at it. She gave me her disgusted annoyed look but continued eating.

A lot of things were affected by the stroke, but not her mind. She remained as alert, intractable, and strong willed as ever. I knew the Pleasant Gardens staff had their work cut out for them.

On one typical Wednesday we were seated at a table for two. I was watching Mom pick at her so-called food and trying to get her to eat everything because maintaining weight is considered crucial. The staff would start giving people supplements if they fell even one pound under their current weight.

"Why do I have to eat so much? I don't like it," she complained.

"Because they want you to. They think it's important for you to keep your weight the same as it's always been."

"I know that; I'm a nurse. So now I can't choose my food and I'm pushed to eat more than I want? It's like the gestapo around here."

There's a saying in hospitals that nurses and doctors make the worst patients. They know too much and want to be in charge of their care.

I sighed. "Please try to eat a little more."

Mom had not met many people since it was a slow time in the rehab section, but she had gotten to know Miriam. Miriam finished her lunch and came clunking over to our table using her walker. Step, step, clunk. Step, step, clunk. Using a walker appeared to require more effort than walking and more coordination, but it was better than the next level of incapacitation — a wheelchair. Miriam was a slight woman with wispy white short hair that floated around her head like a soft cloud. She had a serene smile and exuded an aura of peace and calm acceptance of everything around her, like a saint or a Buddhist monk. She was the opposite of my mother and I hoped Miriam would be a positive influence on Mom.

"So how are you doing, Gertrude?"

"I'm doing pretty well. How about you?"

"I'm doing fine. You're looking well. Better than before."

"No thanks to the food here. I keep trying my best to get well and go home."

"We do the best we can, don't we?"

They reached out and held hands.

"Yes, we do the best we can," agreed my mother with a rare smile.

Miriam had a calming effect on Mom. Since her arrival in Pleasant Gardens, Mom had been, by turns, angry, sad, temperamental, impatient, depressed, determined, courageous, optimistic, and pessimistic. Despite all the conflicting emotions and expectations, she and I were hopeful that her stay in Pleasant Gardens would be over soon and she could go back to her home in Florida.

Miriam's aide was waiting nearby ready to help her to her room. The aide and I exchanged smiles acknowledging the touching scene. These two women had found each other and had begun a friendship of sorts. They were both well educated, well read, and articulate. Miriam was a retired editor. They shared similar backgrounds and experiences having both graduated from college and having had careers, not all that common for women their age. The moment was broken when someone else entered the dining room.

An aide wheeled Michael in. I referred to him as Michael the Morose. He was a dark-haired man with sallow skin who always looked depressed and could barely manage a hello or a smile. I didn't blame him — he was only fifty years old and had had a severe stroke. He couldn't speak very well, and he was in a wheelchair. He was able to use his arms and thus did not need help eating, a definite plus, since assistance for that independent living function was not abundant. Michael had a wife who came every day at lunchtime to keep him company. It was the only time I ever saw him smile. She did all the talking and rattled on enthusiastically filling him in on everyday life at home. I admired her attitude. She was a spark of life in a muted exceptionally quiet place. Her short, burgundy-colored hair was a tangle of curls. Her clothes were lively, too. She favored that bohemian look made up of many layers of different materials and patterns in forms that so overlap you can't tell for sure what articles of clothing they are, but they draped her completely. You'd never know she felt anything but joyful and optimistic. I thought Michael was lucky to have her in his life. Every time I saw her, I was reminded I should try to be more upbeat for mom's sake.

After lunch I pushed my mother's wheelchair back to her room, kissed her goodbye, and left for college. I taught one course in the afternoon and one in the evening, so it was a very long day. It was an hour commute each way and when I got home at ten, despite some snacks at school, all I could think about was eating dinner, which I heated up and gobbled down like a ravenous animal while Jack tried to converse with me. I felt guilty, but after a day spent caring for my mother and then working at the college, combined with my urgent need for food, I could hardly pay attention to what he was saying. To be tired and hungry is not a good scenario for an intimate chat. I promised myself that I would spend more "quality time" with Jack even though I knew that each day was filled with more responsibilities acquired since my mother's stroke.

I began to need naps which I never did before Mom's stroke. I think part of the need for extra sleep was a way to escape some of my new life, post mom's stroke. There were times when I came home from a visit with her and couldn't resist lying down for a snooze, right in the middle of the afternoon. I kept on pushing myself because what choice did I have? I needed to do everything I could to get my mother well and living independently again. She had no one else to do this for her — it had to be me. Melanie cared deeply about our mother, but she lived in faraway Canada. There was only me.

The goal of getting Mom out of the hospital and living on her own again seemed attainable. All I needed to do was keep on going there and encouraging her. I believed it was important to visit every day, so she wouldn't feel alone and wouldn't give up. It became my mission in life.

CHAPTER 7

The Care Plan Meeting

December

Members of the staff had a meeting with Mom and me in her room. It's called a Care Plan meeting and is required by law. The law stipulates that the Care Plan should be "patient centered." I am very familiar with this idea by virtue of my special education experience in writing Individualized Education Plans (IEP's) for each child with a special education classification with the participation of parents and educators in a team meeting. Mom sat in her bed with a somewhat interested, bemused expression on her face and didn't contribute anything to the conversation. It was as though they were exchanging pleasantries rather than discussing her fate. The conclusion they came to was an obvious one — Mom needed to move to the residential center (a.k.a. as a nursing home). Make no mistake about it, a nursing home is not assisted living; it's for people who cannot qualify for assisted living because they are not independent enough.

The therapies had been only minimally successful. She was still unable to walk even after trying so hard. She was able to use her left hand for most things and the right hand to a small degree. She needed assistance with everything. An aide administered her medication at regular times during the day. She required a hospital bed with side rails, so she wouldn't fall on the floor. The staff claimed that my mother was not actually *falling* out of the bed — she was trying to climb right out, and I could believe it. It was the kind of thing my recalcitrant mother would do. I have read that many older adults are treated for bedrail injuries every year. Some people have died after becoming trapped in the rails. There are guidelines for the use of bedrails and the size of openings, but I hadn't heard of any alternative measures for keeping a person in bed. Restraints are not allowed except in limited scenarios when absolutely necessary to treat a resident's medical condition. I was thankful for that because tying a person into their bed must be terrifying and dehumanizing for anyone, but still, I was scared to death she'd fall on the floor and break a hip, that most common of injuries in the elderly. For some reason, when elderly people break a hip, they often die soon after. I discussed this problem, but the team had no ideas on the subject beyond the bedrails.

The three staff members directed their questions to me, and I directed them to address their questions to my mother. They acted like she couldn't possibly comprehend what they were talking about, but I knew she could; she always understood what I said to her. I didn't like the way they were patronizing her by including her physically in the discussion, but not mentally. "My mother is not senile," I told them at one point, "please direct your remarks and questions to her. It's her life we're talking about." She didn't have much to say, though, and mostly just nodded agreeably to the plan set forth. She had become uncharacteristically passive over the last few weeks.

Much as I hated the idea of her living in a nursing home, I felt I had no other choice. I'd visited some assisted living centers, and when I described my mother's needs, I was told she was not a candidate for Assisted Living. She was confined to a wheelchair and needed assistance with all daily living skills. I didn't see how she could come to live with Jack and me, either. Our house had two floors and no bedrooms on the ground floor. The other obstacle was that I was not home, so a fulltime aide would have to be hired. "You'd have to turn your house into a hospital to provide the care she needs," said her doctor. "The cost of providing all that care is exorbitant. Medicare won't pay for it. That's why many people opt for a nursing home placement," he added. "But she can still get better, with time, right?" I persisted. He looked at me silently for a moment and then said it was hard to tell, but a lot of time had gone by with not much recovery of motor skills. He explained it was past the time when spontaneous recovery takes place in stroke patients.

Reluctantly I signed papers to make the change of placement. The federal law pertaining to placement of children with disabilities is guided by the principle of Least Restrictive Environment. I considered this as I agreed to the nursing home placement, but I couldn't think of a less restrictive environment where she would get all the care she needed on a twenty-four hour basis. Doctors insisted that no place else would have the emergency measures in place that she might need given her condition nor the constant surveillance by medical personnel. I realized sadly that the *most* restrictive environment was the only one my mother qualified for.

I still hoped she would recover enough to leave soon.

CHAPTER 8.

Moving Day

Mid December

It was snowing heavily. Great gobs of white were falling fast and furious and covering everything with a blanket of snow. Curbs, bushes, and roads were no longer differentiated from each other in my neighborhood. There were motorist warnings and cars were urged to stay off the roads. It was the day my mother was scheduled to move to the nursing home part of Pleasant Gardens. I wanted to be there so Mom wouldn't be scared or upset, but I knew I couldn't go. I called the front desk.

When the nurse answered, I could hear my mother in the background making her noises. "Unh, unh," she intoned over and over like keeping the beat to some music no one else could hear. She rocked back and forth in time to it. This was a new thing she had started doing and no one could tell me why. The staff often placed her next to the front desk, so she'd have company, but it had no effect on her.

"I'd like to speak to my mother," I said. "She's sitting right in front of you making those sounds."

The nurse put her on the phone. Instantly, Mom stopped making the noises and seemed normal again. The same transformation occurred each time I visited.

"Mom, it's me. I wanted to come today but it's snowing heavily. Looks like a blizzard."

"No, don't come. It's too dangerous."

She sounded like my mother again, always wanting me to be safe. It was reassuring.

"Ok, Mom. I'll come tomorrow to see your new room."

"Ok, Beth. I'll see you then. Stay home."

I believed Mom would grow to like her new living arrangement eventually. I picked Pleasant Gardens because it was close to my house, but also because it was a new, modern building. The décor is all soft colors, new furniture, personal TVs for each resident, and everything is kept clean and neat. The lobby downstairs featured an ice cream bar on weekends, a hair salon, an aviary, pretty murals on the walls, and lots of light. All of that is the kind of thing you would see on a tour. If you were looking for a residential setting for a loved one, you would be impressed by the outward appearance of the place. I was. But I was looking at the wrong things.

I worried that Mom would realize she was in the nursing home section and have a meltdown. But that didn't happen, I was told. She got into the regular routine and was fine except for the rocking and moaning. I hoped she'd stop when she adjusted to her new surroundings. I should have known that was a remote possibility because Mom never adjusted to anything — she always resisted and made things come out her way. This was the first time she wouldn't be able to make that happen. Moving day was the beginning of a gradual loss of control over her own life.

CHAPTER 9

A Crappy Hanukkah

Late December

Mom was in the hospital for ten days with pneumonia. Patients living in residential settings are more likely to get pneumonia due to living in close quarters with so many others. There's even a name for it — Nursing Home Acquired Pneumonia.

She looked so small and pathetic trying to breathe. I felt so sorry for her, that this should have happened to her on top of the stroke and her unhappiness with her new living quarters. The only other time I could remember feeling sorry for her was when Ben died.

The college was closed for the holiday break, and so I was able to visit her in the hospital every day. I went at lunch time and fed her as much as she could eat because the staff told me if she lost weight they would start using the feeding tube dangling from her stomach since the stroke. She was on oxygen part-time. She survived although the doctors and nurses told me they had their doubts that she would. Surprisingly, she gained weight in the hospital. She still looked pale and sickly but was breathing on her own.

"Mom, you're looking so much better. You've gained weight here!"

She gave me her standard sardonic smile. "Of course I have. The food here is better than in that Pleasant Gardens asylum. There's nothing pleasant about it!"

Two days later, the hospital returned her to "the asylum." I visited her that afternoon.

"So, Mom, you look good. How do you feel today?"

"How do you think I feel? Crappy!"

Mom had certain words she used instead of curse words and crappy was one of them. Damn, is the worst word I can ever remember her using. Sometimes she mentioned hell when asking a question about something inexplicable to her like "what the hell was that about?" or "who the hell does she think she is?" The worst name she called people she didn't like was jackass or moron. Her language wasn't racy, but it was uniquely her and expressed her feelings clearly in any situation that arose.

A staff member dressed up like Santa was visiting all the rooms. He brought a smile to her pinched little face with his hearty "Ho, ho, ho," and asked her how she was feeling. She gave him the same answer — crappy. He fished a bottle of body lotion out of his sack (laundry bag) and a Hanukkah teddy bear wearing a yarmulke and handed them to her. "I hope this cheers you up and you feel better each day," he said with a holiday lilt. The way she looked at the fake Santa, like a little child, so happy to have this bit of attention, brought tears to my eyes. I had a Hanukkah present for her, too. I handed her a cuddly stuffed tri-color cat and told her its name was Frisky, just like her real cat Frisky from long ago.

I think she liked the replica of her beloved Frisky as she kept it on her bed for many weeks. It's funny because she never liked any present I bought her, ever. When I began to make money, I bought her beautiful handbags, cashmere sweaters, and once, a necklace of garnets (her birthstone) designed just for her, things she would never have bought for herself. She accepted these gifts with reserved thanks and never used them. Sometimes she gave them back to me, saying she didn't need them, and I should keep them. I felt like I'd been slapped in the face every time, but I kept trying. Now, here was this twenty dollar stuffed animal and she loved it. One day it was gone, and I asked her what happened to it. She looked at me with that sardonic smirk and said, "I gave it away. You know I may be old, but I'm not senile. I don't need toy animals."

Mom passed along her love of animals to Melanie and me. We learned about birth and death by watching our various cats give birth to kittens and losing pets to illness and accidents. Mom invariably had a pet dog or cat and sometimes both at the same time up until she moved to Florida. Once Mom rescued a scrawny, wet, cat stranded on the median of a highway, meowing pitifully in the rain. She stopped the car, got out, scooped it up, and took it home. That cat lived a long and overweight life in my mother's home for many years. Kids in the neighborhood knew Mom was a nurse and compassionate about animals and so they brought wounded birds to her to try and save. She tried. That gift of compassion for animals was one of her best gifts to us and we continued the tradition. We both had pets of our own when we were adults and they were all rescue pets, per Mom's example.

CHAPTER 10.

Traumatic Brain Injury

January

The days I taught classes were the ones I looked forward to the most. As I drove up to the campus and turned into one of the faculty parking lots, I felt the weight of being a caregiver lift off my shoulders and I stood up straighter and walked briskly to the building. I had classes to teach, students to meet with, and meetings to attend with my colleagues. The world of the nursing home disappeared and was replaced by the stimulating environment of the college. When I was there, I hardly thought about Mom, except for one day I remember in particular.

The chapter was Children with Traumatic Brain Injury. "Injury to the brain can cause emotional lability," I told my class of future special education teachers. "It can cause the child to demonstrate mood swings, temper tantrums, inappropriate laughing or crying, impulsivity, hyperactivity, distractibility, depression, and denial of deficits. In addition, there can be decreased physical capabilities, decreased cognitive ability, and loss of speech and language capabilities." I had seen these children in my work in special education and I knew that a stroke is traumatic injury to the brain, but as I was speaking, I recognized my mother in the description and I had to stop reading. It hit me like a brick falling on my head — my mother has traumatic brain injury and it's not just physical impairments; it's all those other characteristics, too, the ones I hadn't been focusing on. She couldn't help many of the personality and behavior changes I was seeing. There was more to her problem than mobility issues. Somehow that had gotten lost in my zeal to see her progress physically. I was putting tremendous effort into seeing that her care in the nursing home was up to the highest standards.

My heart was pounding, and I struggled to recover my composure, but the class must have noticed the sudden silence and began looking at me in a funny way. At the same time as I recognized my mother in the text, I also realized that now I was the 'parent' who would have to be there to advocate for my own parent, just as so many parents of children with disabilities I have known over the years have had to do. How many child study team meetings had I attended where I advised parents to share whatever they wanted to about their child because they knew them best? And how many parents had I advised to fight hard to get the best education they could for their children with special needs? One thing I rarely had to tell them was to love their child and accept them for who they were.

All my teaching and experience had been preparing me for this role, unbeknownst to me. I had seen parents fight tirelessly for their children to be treated with dignity, respect, and proper care and attention and I had aided them in that struggle. And it was a struggle because schools, nursing homes, and institutions in general have specific goals to pursue for their populations, but when things get too difficult or expensive they often renege on or cut back on fulfilling their stated purposes. The populations they work with are vulnerable, powerless people who need advocates more than most. Now it was my turn to be the advocate I had been advising parents to be.

I took a deep breath and hastily closed my book. I explained I had to leave a little early that day. The students began gathering their belongings quietly and giving each other questioning looks. I raced to the parking lot, threw my heavy briefcase in the back seat, and jumped in the car. I arrived at Pleasant Gardens in time to be with Mom during her dinner. At this point I helped her eat when I needed to, but she was doing better at feeding herself. Some progress *is* being made; I had to remind myself.

"Mom, you're doing a good job with that fork, better than last week."

She stopped the fork in midair, smiled, and nodded her head. Then she continued to eat. Tears stung my eyes. She was so grateful to hear my praise. I had forgotten that was part of my job as caregiver, too, just as it had always been for the hundreds of children I had worked with over the years. She *was* doing better, and I had been forgetting to keep on telling her so.

She finished eating her food all by herself. I felt optimism rising within me like a little geyser of hope. I put my arms around her, kissed her, and began to wheel her back to her room. She may not have shown me much physical affection as a mother, but I couldn't stop myself from displaying some affection toward her as a daughter. Despite the lack of overt affection I witnessed as a child, I had grown into a physically affectionate person and behaved that way with my husband and my son. I especially wanted my son to have that in his life.

Mom didn't resist when I leaned over to kiss her.

CHAPTER 11.

Confronting Reality

January

The elevator doors opened, and the stench of urine slapped me in the face like a sour wash rag. My head recoiled involuntarily. I asked one of the aides why it smelled so bad. She said, "It's what happens whenever a bladder infection runs its course on the floor." Later I learned that urinary tract infections are common in nursing homes due to inadequate sanitary precautions, dehydration, and people not being changed on time. Some elderly people become delirious when they have these infections. I ran into one of them on my way down the hall. Rose was a person I always chatted with since she was friendly and usually parked right outside her room which was close to my mother's. I stopped at her wheelchair and said hello. She looked at me with no recognition and spoke to me in a foreign language, I think Yiddish. I said, "Rose, you're speaking Yiddish. Speak English." She continued speaking in the foreign language and looking at me like I was a stranger.

I walked quickly through empty hallways. My mother's room was painted a muted rose color and furnished with a small dresser, a night table, a large orange vinyl chair, and a hospital bed. There were some framed paintings of flowers on the walls and the entire effect was calm and soothing, yet sterile. Maybe it was the white tile floor; so antiseptic. I had arranged some family photos on the dresser next to some of her personal items from home. Directly across from her was her roommate's bed, usually surrounded by the circular aqua curtain that can be drawn for privacy. They shared a bathroom. The last roommate my mother had was Ben. Since his death, she had lived alone and often said she liked it that way and had no interest in living with anyone else, man or woman. I used to ask her if she wanted to date and her response was, "What for? No one can ever replace Ben. Besides, I don't want to wind up being a nursemaid for some decrepit old fool someday." She liked the company of men, and they were attracted to her. She tried dating a few times, but it never went beyond that.

Although Mom didn't complain about the forced roommate situation, I can't imagine suddenly sharing my living space with a stranger, but that's the way the place was set up — there were very few private rooms. The staff insisted this was to encourage socialization, but I think it had more to do with making care easier and more cost effective. My mother's roommate was not much company. Alma was in her nineties and very weak. She stayed in her bed and slept most of the time. She never spoke to my mother or me. I don't think she was aware of much. So much for socialization.

At this point, Mom had been in her new living arrangement for about two weeks. I got her into her wheelchair and pushed her down to the dining room for lunch. She ate pretty well, and I was happy that she had eaten so much of the food given to her, an aspect of her care that was scrupulously monitored. We finished lunch and I pushed the wheelchair back to her room and pulled it up next to her bed. I lifted her under her arms so that she balanced for a second or two on her small feet before I got her into a sitting position on the bed. She couldn't help me in this act, but to wait for an aide always took too long, so I usually did it myself. At five feet three inches in height, my mother only weighed about a hundred fifteen pounds, which was her normal weight, but her dead weight in her limp body felt like a sack of cement. I adjusted the bed, so she was partially sitting up and I placed some new magazines next to her. She lay back on the pillow and I was about to leave when she started to wail and sob and rock her body forward and back, sitting up and down incessantly. No tears flowed but she was distraught.

I'd seen her do this numerous times in the last month or so and it always made me feel guilty and helpless. She moaned, "I want to go home," repeating it over and over desperately, and that progressed into crying jags. I turned on Animal Planet, her favorite afternoon show, but she didn't even glance at it.

"Mom, please stop. You know I can't stay here every minute with you," I said, stating the obvious like an idiot.

"I know," she sobbed.

"I'm here as much as I can be, almost every day. And Melanie comes, and Merwin, and Philip…. we all come and visit as much as we can."

"I know," she said. "They're all good children."

Mom's language was slightly confused. Of the three mentioned, only Melanie is her child and none of them were children anymore, but I was sure she knew who each one was and what their relationship to her was.

"And, Mom, you know you have to stay here for a while. You need lots of care and there's nowhere else you can get it. When you're better you can live somewhere else, but for now, you need to stay here."

She continued rocking back and forth like a human metronome, looking straight ahead, her face twisted in anguish. "I know," she said and then, abruptly stopped rocking, turned, and stared hard at me, "I know, but I don't want to know, Bethanie." I hugged her. Tears stung my eyes. I turned and grabbed the duffle bag filled with her laundry and headed toward the door, so she wouldn't see me cry. I always did her laundry, so her clothes wouldn't get shrunk or lost, common occurrences.

"I'll see you tomorrow," I called and turned to blow her a kiss. She blew one back and finally reclined on her pillow and stayed still. Kissing had reentered our relationship. We kissed each other good-bye every time I left. It just started happening, like it was always part of our lives. I was glad we had this sign of caring and love between us again after all the years that had passed. We needed it now more than ever.

There was no denying it — she really did understand her situation. Until that episode, I wasn't sure. She had probably known for a while and just never wanted to acknowledge it, and now I had forced her to do so, just as I always did in the past, insisting that she see things as they really are, not how she wished they were. Mom could have been the inspiration for the phrase, 'looking at life through rose colored glasses.' She preferred not to talk about difficult things and ignored matters that were uncomfortable for her to discuss. Not real great communication, but when I wanted to talk about something that might be uncomfortable, she always said, "No good can come of it."

I never used to agree with her, but as I get older, I'm beginning to see her point.

CHAPTER 12

Big Ben

My stepfather, Ben, is someone you should know about since he played a role in our dysfunctional family from the time I was nine years old. He was probably the best thing that ever happened to my mother, but I didn't realize it until much later.

Gertrude married Ben at her mother's home in Elizabeth. I recall how she descended the stairs slowly, entered the front hallway, and walked gracefully down the aisle that had been created between the chairs and couches in the living room where about twenty relatives and friends sat. She looked beautiful. Waiting for her at the fireplace under a small portable chuppah was Big Ben and a rabbi.

My sister and I sat in the front row with our grandmother during the ceremony. I was eight years old; Melanie was seven. We hardly knew Ben and had had only a few interactions with him before that ceremony. We were both crying; Melanie, probably because she felt the significance of the moment and everybody else was crying; me, because I wasn't happy and couldn't believe my mother was marrying this man. He had bulging bloodshot eyes, a wide purple nose full of broken veins, a pot belly, and lacked sophistication and education. Everyone referred to Ben as Big Ben because he was a husky guy who had played football in high school. People spoke highly of him, but I couldn't see beyond his appearance and manner. He was not my fantasy father. My ideas about marriage came from watching TV shows and Hollywood movies and were purely romantic. The closest thing to a real marriage on TV was The Honeymooners where the characters fought, yelled at each other vigorously, and made up, but I didn't understand that. I thought they were an exaggeration for comic effect and real marriages were not like that.

Mutual friends had brought the two of them together. Both had been divorced for a few years and they were ready to start anew as a couple. Gertrude was tired of dating and wanted to be in a marriage. Ben was a hardworking plywood salesman, a man with strong family ties, many friends, and no bad habits except cigarette smoking which was not considered a bad habit at the time. Even more importantly to Mom and Grandma, he was Jewish, willing to take on the responsibility of two little girls, and willing to have his new mother-in-law live with them. For Gertrude, he fit the bill. She knew, from experience, there weren't many men like Ben out there. He was a "good man." Everyone described him that way and after her experience with a "bad man" she was ready for a good one. She divorced the "bad man" when I was three and I had no memory of him. My mother told us he was dead, even though he wasn't, and did not allow him into our lives. (I found out he was alive when I was an adult, but that's another story.)

After the wedding, Ben came to live with us in our grandmother's house. It was like having an alien being in our midst. We four females were used to a life without males. We did everything ourselves including painting, repairing, cleaning, cooking, raking, mowing, and anything else that needed doing. I, who had never had a man in my life, began to learn what the opposite sex was like. Ben loved his convertible car, baseball, the New York Post, off color remarks, loud smoke-filled gin games with his pals in our den, and Jewish food.

I resented his intrusion into my life. I know my relationship with him was a disappointment to my mother, but I couldn't accept him. I had no respect for him and could easily prevail in any argument with him on most topics. He had a high school education and seemed narrowminded and prejudiced. Dinnertime was often a battle zone. Mom tried to help him, but it was futile.

What I disliked most about him was his view of his role in the household. He helped in the areas that are traditionally male such as taking out the garbage, mowing the lawn, taking care of the cars, etc. What annoyed and confounded me was his belief that we were there to do everything else. He never cleaned up after himself, never put things away, and never helped with any other household chores. I had never encountered someone who would track mud in the house and ask someone else to clean it up, or who would sit in front of the TV and ask someone to go get him an apple. To put it mildly, I was incensed by his behavior.

I could see that he loved my mother and was good to her, but that made no difference to me. From the day they got married I decided I would never call him Dad as my mother and he wanted. I was an obnoxious stepdaughter, and my non-acceptance of Ben added to the problems between my mother and me. It took many years before I saw the goodness in Ben that everyone else did and could appreciate him and accept his flaws.

CHAPTER 13

Outside Excursions

January

Occasionally, I would take Mom out into the real world, so she could have some stimulation from a source other than Pleasant Gardens. Unless I took her out, she was a prisoner in her new home. Although there were some benches on the premises, no one in a wheelchair could get there without help. I never saw any staff taking residents outside for a walk in the sunshine. They were consumed by all their other responsibilities. Ironically, there was a small putting course which none of the residents were capable of using. When it was warm enough, I would wheel Mom outside to one of the benches so she could feel the sun on her skin. We'd talk or just sit there and watch squirrels and birds that happened by. It seemed a cruel punishment to be deprived of exposure to the outdoors and nature so I tried to make up for it when I could.

I took Mom out for trips to the mall or a park or to a restaurant whenever I could. Pleasant Gardens did none of that. When I asked why they didn't rent a van or a bus and take the residents anywhere off the premises, they said it was too expensive, too difficult, and too risky. I was familiar with the idea of protecting people with disabilities from risky undertakings, but that caution was tempered by the special education philosophy of "the dignity of risk." Educators have come to understand that too much protection and paternalism erodes one's sense of competence. Life involves a certain amount of risk taking or we'd all be living in bubbles. I wished that Pleasant Gardens ascribed to that philosophy. I understood their need to protect their charges, but I'm sure that liability also played a role. Local outsiders were brought in on occasion to entertain but the residents didn't get out.

On this particular day, I thought the mall would be especially cheery since Christmas decorations were still up. After transferring her from the portable wheelchair to the car seat, I strapped her in, folded up the wheelchair and stowed it in the trunk. It was cold, and my mother looked like a child wearing my too-large powder-blue ski jacket with the hood up. Mom got rid of such cold weather items when she moved to Florida. At the mall, I went through the reverse process of getting her out of the car and into the wheelchair. I'm not a big person and lifting her was extremely difficult for me, but there was no way around it. My back had begun to protest, and I hoped I wasn't doing damage to it. At night I took pills to relieve the aching.

There were still Christmas decorations throughout the mall and in the stores. The scent of holiday candles wafted out of the smaller stores and Christmas music still played on the audio system. The sales were on, and I guess the stores all thought promoting the Christmas spirit would help customers remain in a holiday mood and spend money. We looked around in Macy's, but Mom was not interested in looking at any clothes for herself. "You look, Beth, I'll just watch you," she said. And so I did, eventually buying a sweater on sale, more to entertain her than because I wanted it. This was a new activity for her — vicarious shopping. She used to love to buy clothes for herself (at bargain stores of course,) but now, she had no use for new clothes and knew it. So many of the joys of her former life were gone, this was just one more.

We strolled around for about an hour when she said, "I'm getting a little bored."

"Do you want to go back to Pleasant Gardens?"

"I think so. I'm all tuckered out."

We headed back to the place I thought she was dying to get away from. I was in the hall on my way out as the aide was getting her into her bed and I overheard her ask my mother, "How was your visit to the mall with your daughter?"

"It stank." said my mother. "But she thinks I liked it."

I realized that I had just expended an immense amount of effort for nothing.

She never seemed to enjoy all these outings and that was disappointing, but I guess I didn't realize how much my mother had changed. I noticed that she never suggested going out anywhere and our visits to the nail salon, restaurants, shops, etc., were never the exhilarating experience I hoped for. During her last pedicure, she fell asleep and when she woke up, was startled to see her toenails painted a bright holiday red. I was beginning to think that maybe I should accept that she was just not interested in a lot of things anymore.

It was ironic that I had become so involved in my mother's life because, looking back I never felt my mother was involved in shaping my life; only in reacting to it. She never seemed interested in what I did unless it turned out wrong. I observed how extensively my friends' mothers participated in their daughters' lives, guiding them, and insinuating themselves into all that they did, sometimes on a moment by moment basis, and I craved that attention. I don't recall any interest on her part in my schoolwork or future aspirations. Her parenting philosophy was making me obey her rules, which were many. She did take us to Disney Land once and that was a highlight of my childhood. After she married Ben, her social life became her focus. They went out with friends every Saturday night, played cards with them, and spent time with them at the swim club. What Melanie and I did was up to us within restrictions.

I think I just grew up like a weed, untended but somehow strong and defiant, determined to grow though not always in the best direction.

CHAPTER 14.

Fun and Games at Pleasant Gardens

January

"Bethanie, can we dance our way out of here?" Since her stroke, my mother had been expressing herself in strange ways, but I usually knew what she meant. She could articulate clearly but had difficulty finding words. We were sitting in the activity room of in Pleasant Gardens and Rusty, the social director, was leading a group of the residents in his version of musical chairs. All twenty residents present, including my mother, were in wheelchairs arranged in a circle. It reminded me of circling the wagons in a Western movie. The game consisted of passing a ball to the person next to you in time to music playing on a cassette player. When Rusty's assistant stopped the tape, the person holding the ball got to do a little dance with Rusty, while seated, and then he pushed their wheelchair out of the circle. Musical wheelchairs, what a concept. Quite a few of the residents had trouble passing the ball to the person next to them and when they dropped it, Rusty rushed over and handed it to the person waiting for it. I thought it was embarrassing for the person who dropped the ball because they knew it shouldn't be a hard task. My feeling was, if you're going to play a stupid game, at least make it one that fits the capabilities of the participants.

I looked at the people in their wheelchairs, expressionless, as Rusty kept up his nonstop patter. He didn't engage with them, except as part of his recreational plan. I felt sad as I watched and couldn't help thinking, all these people have past lives, and no one takes the time to remember them. They were parents, grandparents, business owners, professionals, others who worked in trades and blue collar jobs, or maybe never worked. They came from all kinds of backgrounds, yet these were no longer acknowledged. Here, they had lost their identities, a profound loss.

My mother found the whole musical chairs thing inane as she did most of Rusty's activities and was impatient to leave. "Rusty is a jackass," she said without lowering her voice. "Get me out of here." She was never a patient person, but since her stroke, her tolerance threshold for waiting was even lower. Waiting of any kind made her agitated. She would start rocking, tapping her feet, and looking around incessantly. Eventually she would start asking questions in a loud aggressive tone such as, "What the hell is taking so long?" and "How long does a person have to wait around here?" This behavior was not typical of her before the stroke.

"But, Mom, soon they'll be serving cake and juice. Don't you want to wait till then?"

My mother was always a big cake fan. She used to bake them often and loved inventing her own versions of them. She gave me one of her perturbed expressions scrunching up one side of her mouth and narrowing her eyebrows but seemed willing to stick around a little longer.

At last musical wheelchairs was over and the aides passed out The Afternoon Snack. On this day it was yellow cake with white frosting served on flimsy paper plates with tiny plastic forks. The residents tried to eat the cake while holding the floppy plates in their laps and manipulating child-sized forks. Of course, it was a mess and there were only a couple of aides to help them. It's a good thing I was there to help my mother since her right arm still wasn't functioning and she had to eat with her left hand, something she was just getting accustomed to. It was a two-handed job, no matter how you looked at it, because of balancing the plate. Usually snacks were served at tables in the dining room, but Rusty wanted to play this game, so he had the snack served in the activity room.

"This is boring cake," announced my mother, the inventor of far more interesting cakes; a person who would never have put vanilla frosting on a yellow cake. She was making chocolate/pecan frosting by doctoring canned frosting before anyone else thought of it, she'd have you know.

"They need to get a new banana, too. He's not a very good dancer," declared my mother, oblivious of cake crumbs clinging to her mouth and chin.

I think she was referring to Rusty using an old expression, top banana, which was used in her day to refer to an emcee. I got the message and rolled her away. After snack time, most of the residents would go back to their rooms to watch TV and/or take a nap. Some preferred to hang out around the nurses' station and ended up dozing there. They rarely talked to each other and communicated mostly with the staff or their visitors. Forced socialization was almost the only kind of socialization I observed. People didn't ride around in their wheelchairs seeking each other out in the public spaces or each other's rooms. They interacted minimally during the daily activities if at all. I guess they didn't aspire to making new friends, because they were all severely debilitated and just lived from pill to pill and meal to meal.

There were activities every day, but my mother gave up on them after a few brief trials. As she put it, "if I wanted to make stupid crafts or play insipid bingo, I would have been doing it before. These activities are designed for morons." The daily activities included putting together large puzzles, current event discussion groups where few people added to what the discussion leader had to say, and arts and crafts. Treating the elderly like children was a rampant practice. It wasn't only the nature of the activities; it was the way the staff spoke to the residents, too. They all sounded like kindergarten teachers.

CHAPTER 15.

Driving Lessons

January

After helping her with a meal I often gave Mom a "driving lesson" which is what I called practice using her wheelchair. Right after lunch was sort of dead time. Most of the residents were toileted and then took naps. I didn't want my mother to just drift off into sleepy-time-land every day, so sometimes I gave her a "driving lesson." She couldn't roll anywhere independently because she wasn't able to maneuver the wheels with her hands, either due to lack of strength or something else, I don't know, but I knew she needed to be able to move around on her own to feel some freedom and control over her circumstances. They didn't allow motorized wheelchairs for safety reasons, I was told.

My goal was to have her pull herself along using her strong left hand on the handrail in the hallways, while using her right hand to push on the right wheel. Up and down the halls we went with me pushing her as lightly as possible hoping that any minute she'd take off and be moving along under her own power. It reminded me of teaching a child to ride a two-wheeler. I would wait expectantly for that moment when she was rolling under her own steam, and I could recede into the background and watch her go. But it never happened.

She seemed to like our training sessions and got a really determined look on her face as she pulled herself along the wall like a snail in a fish tank. She always wanted to go faster so I pushed a little more.

"We're having our driving lesson!" I would call cheerily, which is how I said everything since her move to Pleasant Gardens. "It's not the Mercury Marquis, but we're moving," I'd say.

Mom would turn her head to look up at me, smirk, and give me her are-you-kidding look, but I could tell she was enjoying herself because she didn't ask me to stop. After a while, she would say she was tired and wanted to go back to her room.

"Mom, you're doing better today," I would lie.

"Yeah, I think so too. Maybe soon I'll be able to drive my car again."

"I hope so, Mom."

I didn't have the heart to tell her that I had sold her car weeks ago when I realized we were in for a long haul. The insurance and the car payments were a drain on her funds. The money was better utilized in her bank account to pay the costs of the nursing home. She could always buy another car in the future if she was ever in the condition to drive again, I reasoned. Until then, traversing the halls in her wheelchair would have to be the extent of her driving.

Mom always loved driving. I remember when I was twelve, she packed us all; me, Melanie, Ben, Grandma, and our orange cat, into the family car and drove across the country to Arizona to visit Merwin and his family. The cat sat on the back of the driver's seat the whole way. We had to sneak him into our motel rooms at night. Mom did most of the driving and Ben helped somewhat — he didn't love the idea of the cat wrapped around the back of his neck like a fur collar for hours. After she retired, she began making her annual pilgrimage from Florida to New Jersey and then, continuing on to Canada. She had no qualms about driving up and down the entire East coast. She preferred the flexibility it gave her for arrivals and departures and, once she got to her destination, she never had to rent a car. Buses, trains, and planes held no appeal for her. She was a bit of a speed demon and liked to zoom along on Interstate 95 doing about eighty. She was planning on driving back to Florida as usual when the stroke occurred. Over the years, my sister and I begged her to get a cell phone, but stubborn Gertrude said she didn't need one. She also refused to consider suggestions that she fly and send the car up with a driver. She had no interest in the auto train either. On the contrary, she enjoyed each trip.

Mom was a no-frills driver and eschewed books on tape, CD's, and all those other distractors. If she couldn't find any classical music on the radio, she went cold turkey — just her and the road. I'm sure other drivers steered clear of the petite auburn-haired woman with the intense expression and the white knuckled grip on the steering wheel, racing along the highway in a big white car, like Moby Dick tearing through the ocean in a single-minded mood. She loved her Mercury Marquis and bought the same model in white every few years. The huge trunk held all the clothes and personal items she would need for the next five months. I liked the fact that it was a big car and probably safer. I always worried that she'd have an accident, but she never did and never got lost either. That Mercury Marquis knew exactly the route to take and never failed her. "I just point it toward New Jersey, and it knows the way," she would say.

CHAPTER 16.

Big Ben in Retrospect

came to appreciate my stepfather slowly, like an acquired taste. He was not the father I had dreamed of, but I began to see that he was a buffer between my mother and me. Although he entered our lives when I was nine, I didn't recognize the importance of his role in my life until I was twelve. I wanted an English Racer bike, and my mother was opposed. Her response was, "the Schwinn is good enough." Everyone was getting these new slim black bikes with handbrakes and wire spokes while I was stuck riding my clunky, rusty Schwinn with footbrakes and fat tires. I wanted to have the kind of bike all the other kids were getting. They went faster and looked much cooler. None of this mattered to Mom. One day Ben told us to look in the garage, there was a surprise there. Melanie and I could hardly believe our eyes; there stood two shiny, sleek, black English racers. I'm not sure how he pulled this off since I never heard them talking about it. I knew it was his idea.

I began to see that he wanted to be a father to us, but he was not encouraged to do so. Mom made all the decisions about us. She ruled the home front and argued with Ben almost as much as with me. Her automatic response to everything was to oppose whatever you were saying and insist that you were wrong, and she was right. These were not calm discussions. She would get angrier and angrier if you didn't agree with her and yelling would begin. Mom's arguments with Ben were not restricted to consequential family matters; they could just as easily be about politics, religion, or money. Often Ben wanted to lend money to a friend on hard times or donate money to a synagogue or a Jewish charity, and this propensity for generosity caused some of their biggest arguments. My mother was not interested in "giving our money away." They rarely agreed on anything. When things got ridiculously heated, Ben would try to put on the brakes and laugh and say, "Aw, Gertie, you always have to have the last word." Immediately she would respond, "Yes, I do."

I never saw her initiate physical affection with him. She would pull away when he came up behind her and put his arms around her while she was doing the dishes or cooking. She'd laugh and wriggle out of his grip. I know she cared about him, but her relationship with him was not the role model for a happily married couple. Ben was like a giant puppy looking for a pat on the head. Eventually, I felt sorry for him and wished he would stand up to her more. But he was not a fighter; he was a lover, and he loved her.

The junior prom incident was another one that stands out in my mind as an example of Ben going to bat for me. I was forbidden to date non-Jewish boys, but I did. I kept it secret until I started "going steady" with an Irish kid. Jerry was cute in a freckled, red haired, Irish way, with an upturned nose like a leprechaun, and a mischievous grin. What I liked most about him was his sense of humor. He could make anything seem funny. We were dating all during my Junior year and consequently, unlike some girls, I knew I had a date for the Junior Prom, a big deal in my high school. When I told Mom I was going to the Prom with Jerry, she had a conniption. "You're not going to the Prom with him, a gentile. You find a Jewish boy or stay home." "But Mom, you can't mean that. Everyone goes to the Prom. I can't just find a Jewish date at this point. Besides, you know I've been dating Jerry all year. I can't leave him high and dry." She knew he was my boyfriend but chose to ignore it. When Jerry was in our home, she was barely civil to him.

We were in the middle of a screaming match with me crying and Mom resolutely maintaining her position when I noticed Ben had come into the room. He stood a few feet behind my mother and said in a tired pleading voice, "Aww, Gertie, just let her go." She turned around, looked at him in astonishment, and left the room in a huff. She was as surprised as I was that he had intervened. Ben didn't want me dating any boys but Jewish ones either, so this was a real compromise on his part. The next day, Mom acquiesced. Ben was my savior in this instance and others as time went on. He often said my mother and I were like oil and water.

I really got to know who my stepfather was when he lost his driver's license for a month. I don't remember what the offense was, but for a traveling salesman it was a harsh punishment and an impossible situation. It was summer, I was seventeen, and I was pressed into service as his chauffeur. We spent many hot days in his unairconditioned car, windows wide open, driving all over the farmlands of Jersey where his clients had their businesses. They were mostly cabinet makers and home builders. When he wasn't listening to baseball games on the radio, we talked. Ben was six when his Orthodox Jewish family left Austria for America. I listened to his stories of pogroms in Europe, Cossacks riding through his town, and later being beaten up by Christian kids in the schools and neighborhoods of New Jersey. I began to understand why he felt so strongly about the Jewish people — he had endured antisemitism most of his life.

During that sweltering summer, I saw first-hand how hard his job was, trying to sell plywood to men who could buy it elsewhere.

He used all the ploys he could think of from flattery to hard negotiating, to downright begging. He reminded these men of their history together over the years and made them feel guilty not buying from him, their "good friend." "How can you do this to me?" he'd say. And often, they couldn't. It was exhausting work and when he got home he always drank a shot of whiskey and leaned back in his easy chair to read The New York Post before dinner. This was his life, and he did it for us. I got it. That experience was maybe the first Take-Your-Daughter-to-Work Day except it lasted a month.

When Ben's kidneys gave out and he went on dialysis, it drained his health and his spirit. He dragged himself around, listless, weak. Other medical problems began to surface and after a lot of suffering he was in the hospital and eventually in a coma. During this period, I saw the love my mother had for him. She may not have been overtly affectionate, but she was a fabulous nurse/wife. She was in the hospital every day overseeing his care and holding his hand while Ben lay silently in bed with his eyes closed. She talked to him because some doctors told her he might be listening, and it might stimulate him. When a nurse softly suggested to me that I persuade my mother to take Ben off life support, my mother overheard. I never had to answer because Gertrude turned into a cyclone and let that nurse know in a voice filled with rage, tears streaming down her cheeks, that no one was ever going to "pull the plug" on her husband. He died peacefully not long after with her by his side.

It took me a long time to see Ben as everyone else saw him: a good guy. Not rich, not debonair, not well educated or well spoken, but a man who thought with his heart. He understood people; he didn't need a Ph.D. in human relations, he came by it naturally. The obnoxious stepdaughter and the much maligned and long-suffering stepfather forged a bond later in life and when he died, I was bereft.

CHAPTER 17

Gertrude's Psychiatric Evaluation

February

decided to consult with a doctor of the mind to find out if my mother's behavior was a result of the stroke or her unhappiness about her new situation or something else. She was still making repetitive noises and rocking in her wheelchair with what appeared to be involuntary momentum. Sometimes she looked like she was in a stupor and just stared into space seemingly oblivious of everything and everybody including me. At other times she was pretty normal. It was like being on a roller coaster riding her moods never knowing which Gertrude I'd encounter.

I wanted to find out if she was competent mentally or was showing signs of senility or Alzheimer's. I felt I couldn't ask her to make decisions and sign things until I found out. Although I had power of attorney, it is a huge responsibility to make decisions for someone else and I was not comfortable doing it especially when she seemed lucid much of the time. I hadn't noticed anything like what I would call senility, but there was no doubt that she seemed confused at times. Often, she referred to herself in the third person. I would ask her a question like do you want to do such and such and she would answer, 'she doesn't.' It was strange and I felt like I was talking to her representative, not her. I didn't know how much of this behavior was related to the stroke or something else, but I did know my mother had changed.

The other thing I wanted to get a handle on was her medications. Since he was a psychiatrist, Dr. Gelb could prescribe some meds that might work better than what she'd been getting. Apparently the medical staff at Pleasant Gardens, with input from the staff psychologist, was allowed to make changes whenever they felt it was necessary. I was never asked permission nor told the results of their evaluations. The doctor on staff made changes in the medications and Medicare was billed. I was told this was standard procedure. Something seemed amiss here since no one on the patient side of the equation participated in these decisions.

I asked the head nurse about my mother's staring; unresponsive behaviors and I was told it could be due to the change in meds. When I asked what changes specifically, she answered huffily I was free to look at my mother's chart and see what medications she was on at any time. Lots of luck understanding those charts, I thought. I noticed one medication that I had heard of and Googled it. According to the websites, it's an anti-anxiety drug which may have side effects of confusion, hyperactivity, hallucinations, depression, agitation; in short, a lot of the behaviors I'd observed in my mother since her arrival at Pleasant Gardens. Further investigation on the web revealed that there is concern that too many nursing homes use drugs of this type to subdue patients and control their behavior. When I read this, I was incensed and determined to have someone, other than Pleasant Gardens staff, overseeing her meds.

And so, on a freezing cold February day, we went to see Dr. Gelb, a middle-aged, handsome man with turquoise eyes set in a tanned face like jewels on a sandy beach. He was wearing what looked like an expensive Italian suit and elegant tan leather loafers, probably also Italian. Everything had that slim, fitted, European look including him. Personally, I was hoping for an older doctor; someone who looked more like Freud. He built some rapport with my mother by talking about the frigid weather outside, and some other mundane things before sliding into his evaluation. He asked her how she liked Pleasant Gardens and she answered it was okay. Dr. Gelb thought it would be helpful if I stayed in the room. Mom didn't mind at all.

"So, Gertrude, how old are you?" he asked.

Unbelievably, my mother hesitated and appeared to be thinking hard. This was something I never asked her; I just took it for granted she knew.

"Ninety?" she ventured.

I was aghast. It was such an easy question. How would she do on the rest?

"And Gertrude," continued the psychiatrist appearing unsurprised by her answer, "who is this sitting next to you?"

My mother smiled. "That's my daughter, Bethanie."

I was so relieved. But the next question did not go as well.

"And what was the name of your husband?" continued the doctor in his oh-so-casual manner.

"Leo."

Another shocker! She had always avoided mentioning him. They had only been married for about four years. It was Ben I expected her to answer, her spouse for thirty years. The doctor and I exchanged looks because he knew nothing about Leo. His background information listed only Ben. Quickly I wrote him a note: first husband.

"Was he your only husband?" continued the charming doctor.

"Yes. He was a good man; everyone said he was a good man." I was convinced Mom was talking about Ben but calling him Leo. She had been confused about family members' names since the stroke. Her statement about him being a good man is something she and everyone used to say about Ben, and I was sure she would never describe Leo as a good man. She despised him so much she refused to talk about him most of her life.

"Do you ever think of wanting to die?"

"No, never!" my mother answered adamantly. I knew this to be a fact as she could not be persuaded to draw up a living will, giving the excuse that she had no intention of dying, ever. It was her way of avoiding, once again, an unpleasant topic.

"Do you understand that you had a stroke?"

"Yes, possibly, before the accident."

Things were getting increasingly confused. Apparently, my mother still thought she had had an accident and did not comprehend that her problems were due to a stroke. She knew very well what a stroke is and what it can do — she was a nurse.

I couldn't believe I'd never noticed all this confusion. Of course, I'd never asked her those kinds of questions. Why would I? The doctor asked to talk to me privately and my mother said that was fine with her. For a person who had always insisted on having complete control of her life, she had, over the past few months, become amazingly willing to let me take over.

"I get the impression your mother is a very intelligent woman and a very social one. Throughout our interview she seemed to be enjoying our conversation."

"Oh, yes," I agreed. "My mother is smart and highly educated as you can see from her background papers. She is very social and has always had a lot of good friends."

He shared some other impressions of her and said she did not show signs of Alzheimer's but, there was definitely confusion.

"So, do you think she is mentally competent? Can she make decisions and sign papers that might be needed in the future?" I was thinking of a living will or some medical treatment.

"Are you joking?" the doctor said. "No, she cannot make decisions or sign papers on her own behalf. Surely you can see that she is not capable mentally of doing that."

He sounded perturbed that I would even ask such a thing. I felt like an idiot and a chastised child at the same time. We moved on to my concerns about the medications and he told me he was changing her medications and it might have a positive effect on her behavior, but he was not optimistic about it improving her cognitive functioning. He said she was showing early signs of dementia which happens sometimes to people in their eighties. My mother, demented. I found this hard to believe, but the interview was an eye opener to say the least.

Mom was in great spirits out in the waiting room.

"Isn't he just the handsomest man?" she exclaimed.

"Yes, he is. He's going to change some medications for you, and I think you'll feel better."

"I feel better already," she said beaming. "When can we talk to him again?"

All during the interview I had the feeling that she was being just a little bit coquettish. Mom was taken with the good-looking doctor, no doubt. He certainly was a change of pace from the denizens of Pleasant Gardens. My mother was always charming and conversational, especially with men, and liked to flirt with them and get them to do special things for her. Many a repair man, landlord, or salesman went out of his way for my mom. She had a way about her, even at eighty-four.

CHAPTER 18.

Mom's Hidden Past

For many years, Mom kept her past a secret. She always told Melanie and me that our father was dead. I had never seen a picture of him anywhere. She shared that they had met in the armed forces when she was serving as a nurse and he as a pilot during WW II. I pressed for more information; however, Mom was not forthcoming. It was not until I was about eight and, while rooting around in her desk, as curious children will do, I stumbled on her divorce papers from Leo. I confronted her immediately. She coolly brushed it aside saying, "Yes we were divorced. I never told you because it was just easier not to talk about that painful episode." I asked if he was still alive. She answered that he died right after the divorce.

She had lied to me once, therefore, I lost trust in her account of the past. If my father was still alive, I wanted to meet him. A few years later, after more annoying questions from me, Mom shared that they had gotten divorced because he was a Baptist, and she found his religion in conflict with her Judaism as their marriage progressed. I believed her. When I asked if maybe he was alive, she responded, "I don't know or care and if you're smart, you won't try to find him because he was a bad man." Then I wasn't sure if I still wanted to meet him. Why would I want to open the door to a relationship with a "bad man"?

The final revelations didn't occur until I was in college and visiting her and Ben in Florida. I was looking through a family photo album. Ben was out for a walk, and Mom was busy in the kitchen making tuna fish for lunch. When she was done, she came into the living room and sat next to me on the beige puffy sofa, one of the pieces of furniture from my grandmother's living room. It still felt wrong to be sitting on it since I had never been allowed to as a child. She smiled and pointed to a black and white photo of herself and another woman wearing army nurse uniforms.

'Oh, that's me and Jeanette. We were in England.'

"Why did you enlist?" I asked her.

"I was fresh out of nursing school and had been working at Bellevue in the psyche ward. The patients there were scarier than the Nazis. One by one, the men I knew enlisted. My best friend, Jeanette, and I decided to enlist, too. My parents didn't want me to go, but I went anyway."

My mother the rebel, a person I never knew. She turned the page and browsed through the fuzzy, gray photos. Some were taken in Tampa, where I knew she had lived with Leo when Melanie and I were babies. Now seemed like a good time to probe just a little. I asked her again about the man I had wondered about for so long.

"How did you meet Leo?"

I waited for her to get angry, but she was in a different, unexpected mood. A slight smile played on her lips.

"We met at an officer's club in England. Captain Leo Carpenter was having a drink with his flier buddies when a fast jitterbug began playing and the couples on the floor began to really swing. I was dancing with a friend, a good dancer, and I was pretty good myself. Afterwards, Leo came over and introduced himself. And that was it. We fell in love." Mom had a faraway, dreamy look on her face.

'So then what happened," I persisted.

"Our relationship progressed swiftly as most did during the war. We never knew if we would see each other again each time we parted. But we survived and then got married over my parents' objections. They did not want me marrying a Christian." She turned to me and said softly, "He was the love of my life." Quickly she looked away again.

I was dumbstruck. My mother never talked this way, ever. I asked what happened next.

"Leo began wanting to take you girls to church. I didn't want that. But the bigger issue was his unrest. He wanted to go back to being a pilot and I was afraid for him to do that. I refused to let him. Eventually, he had an affair and I left him." She stood up abruptly saying it was time for lunch.

After that conversation, I knew that I would search for Leo because he might be alive. I still had a need to meet my biological father if possible.

It was many years later, and I was a married woman with a son, when I found him and flew to Florida to meet him. We spent a long weekend getting to know each other. I was impressed by the history he shared with me. He was incredibly brave, a war hero, and a man who fell head over heels in love with my mother. He took full responsibility for the breakup of their marriage calling himself weak and very unhappy at the time. He said that after the divorce he had wanted to have a relationship with his daughters, but Mom and my grandmother made it impossible.

Meeting him was one of the most important things I've done in my life, and I've never regretted it, despite the fact that I didn't feel the need to continue our relationship after that. Too much time had elapsed, and it was too late, I felt. Leo agreed. We both had our own families and our separate family histories. I felt that at his age he deserved to live the happy, well respected life he had created without interference from me. For me, the missing piece of who I was and where I came from was put into place. I never saw him again. He wrote me a beautiful letter about how much it had meant to him to meet me. He said he would have his family notify me when he died, and they did.

That weekend I found not only my father — I found a mother I never knew. She was fearless and determined to live her life as she desired despite parental objections. She was swept away by love and then crushed by the loss of that love. She pulled herself together and went back to New Jersey, moved in with her mother, and began working fulltime as a nurse.

While I wasn't happy that she had prevented me from knowing my father, I understood how she felt and how much she wanted to put the past behind her and start over. By the time I met Leo, I understood how complex and painful that period of time was for her. My reaction was quite different from what it might have been had I found him when I was younger. I could visualize them as two young people who fell in love while both serving their country in a foreign land. They tried to make the marriage work but didn't succeed. I was able to see them as they were long ago and did not judge them. They were just human beings who made mistakes like we all do.

CHAPTER 19.

Filling in Time

February

My daily visits usually followed a pattern of helping Mom eat her lunch, or dinner, depending on when I could get there, and then spending time with her, wheeling her around either inside or outside around the grounds. There was an aviary downstairs in the main lobby where brightly colored small birds, finches mostly, flitted about, cheeping, pecking at their seeds, and going nowhere, but we'd seen them so many times, it was no longer appealing. I didn't like to look at the aviary because I felt sorry for the birds caged behind glass their entire lives, never allowed to fly in the sky. It reminded me of the residents, prisoners in their isolated world, cut off from others of their species. I read that the average nursing home stay is two years and most of the people who enter in their eighties, die there. The finches were certainly going to die in their tiny glass universe eventually.

When she first moved in, I would push her wheelchair up one hallway and down another. There was artwork on the walls; framed pictures of flowers, outdoor scenes, fruit, and more of the same ilk — nothing interesting. They were selected for décor, not artistic merit and Mom was as bored by them as I was. When Melanie and I were young children, she took us to the museums of New York City. She knew her artists and taught us about them. It is because of that early exposure that my sister and I both enjoy art today.

Outside, if it was good weather, I'd take her on the path surrounding Pleasant Gardens. After circling the building once, you'd seen everything there was to see. Pleasant Gardens was off a busy road dotted with a few small strip malls, medical offices, and a hospital. There were no sidewalks and traffic on the main road was fast and heavy. Excursions in her wheelchair were therefore limited to the grounds surrounding the facility which consisted mostly of lawns, some seating areas, and beyond that, woods. There were few flowers in the landscaping and no gardens, despite the name. The fresh air was the real benefit and sometimes we just sat outside on a bench and relaxed in the sun.

When it was close to Valentine's Day, the daily activity was making valentines out of colored paper and lace, just like I used to do in elementary school. Of course, Mom wasn't the least bit interested. Besides, her impaired fine motor skills prevented her from performing any of the necessary skills needed like using scissors or a pencil.

I brought cards and letters from her friends, and we read them. All of them still lived in Florida so they couldn't visit. They missed their "Gertie" and filled her in on the doings down there in retirement land. We looked at magazines together. This was just one more thing she could no longer do on her own. She couldn't hold the magazine and turn the pages, so that had become another "activity" that we did together. I bought subscriptions to her favorite magazines, *Family Circle* and *Good Housekeeping*. I used to bring family photo albums along, but her interest in them waned after a while, or was it too painful remembering how she used to be? All I know is, she lost interest in that activity.

Mom used to love to read, but she couldn't anymore. I acquired my love of reading from her, and it is one of the best gifts she ever gave me. She got me a library card when I was in the first grade. She read to my sister and me every night before bedtime until we were able to read our own books. She started with the easy picture books and invested in a slew of Little Golden Books that sat on a bookshelf in the bedroom I shared with my sister. As we got older, she moved on to longer books. I still remember her sitting on the bedside reading a chapter to us from *Heidi* or *The Wizard of Oz* or *Treasure Island* each night until the book was finished. I don't know how she knew what the children's classics are, but that is where her tastes led us. She introduced us to *Pippi Longstocking*, *Grimm's Fairy Tales*, *Hans Christian Anderson's Fairy Tales*, *Mary Poppins*, *Caddie Woodlawn*, and *Peter Pan*. I was familiar with them all long before they were movies or Broadway musicals. By the time I was in seventh grade, Mom and I were often reading the same books and she never told me they were too adult for me or that I wouldn't understand them. If she was reading a book, I'd check it out and, if it interested me, I'd read it. My eighth grade teacher once questioned why I submitted a book report on a book that was too adult for me. It was *Something of Value* by Robert Ruark and had sex and violence in it and was set during the Mau Mau uprising in Kenya. I told my mother that the teacher had questioned my book choice. That teacher got an earful as my mother yelled into the phone that she should be encouraging me to read at higher levels since I was capable and that the book was one she approved of. Then she called the teacher a moron for extra emphasis. I got an "A" on the book report.

Traversing the halls of the nursing home, Mom liked to tuck a book next to her hip in the wheelchair and if people asked her about it, she told them how much she was enjoying it. I functioned as her personal librarian and brought her selections from the public library that I thought she might like. She always liked historical best sellers, stories involving travel, family sagas, anything by Rosamunde Pilcher, Penelope Fitzgerald, and anything with a talking or deep-thinking cat (there are quite a few of those). We didn't discuss her loss of reading ability. We functioned as if she could read. Again, my mother's philosophy of not talking about the distressing aspects of life made sense in this situation. I understand the Asian philosophy of face saving now more than I ever have, and I tried to save face for Mom as much as possible. Sometimes there are no benefits to telling the truth.

I think it would have been better for her if she *were* senile, so she wouldn't have been so aware of all her new limitations. For a woman with a very sharp mind, her new life was a constant confrontation with what she had lost.

CHAPTER 20

Medication as Behavior Modification

February

My mother was one of the problematic residents at Pleasant Gardens. She yelled and cried when she was unhappy, and she let the staff know how she felt about the whole experience of being in a nursing home. She resisted their efforts to get her involved in their activities and follow their schedule. I noticed that my Mom was staring off into space at times; not eating or talking, not reacting to stimuli normally. It was as if she'd had a lobotomy. I'd arrive, and she'd stare at me blankly. One day, I checked her chart to see if the medications were the ones Dr. Gelb had prescribed. They were not. I freaked out. I found the head nurse and asked why Dr. Gelb's prescriptions were no longer being administered. She stopped looking at her charts, looked up at me with disdain for a moment, then at her charts again. She refused to have eye contact as she responded to me.

"We asked our doctor to review her medications in light of her continuing difficult behavior. He prescribed some new medications to help your mother calm down."

"Who authorized these changes?"

"The head physician and psychologist here at Pleasant Gardens." Then she looked straight at me with a penetrating stare that felt like needles and continued, "We can't call the family and get permission to change medications to meet individual needs as we observe them. That would mean residents would not get the medication they need when they need it. That's why your mother is in our care — so we can take care of her. It would not be feasible to call you and explain what medication your mother needs or doesn't need. We are constantly managing her meds according to her changing needs." She gave me a thin, tight lipped smile and walked away.

I never liked the head nurse. Everything she said was through compressed lips that barely moved. It was like her jaw was wired. There was nothing but coldness in her demeanor. I felt contempt emanating from her in icy waves whenever I made her stop her work and answer my questions. It was clear to me that if a patient was causing too much trouble or required too much attention, they were sedated. This was not a new approach to me; I'd seen it used with children with disabilities who are hard to handle, too. It's a quick fix and not recommended by any authorities in gerontology or special education.

I tried to save Mom from overmedication by getting Dr. Gelb's evaluation, but it didn't last. My mother was at their mercy, under their total control. I admit my mother was hard to manage, and her moaning and crying were irritating and disturbing to everyone, but I didn't see that as a justification for drugging her to the point of oblivion. After that incident, I noticed that Mom was more normal again. Maybe they listened to me after all and reduced the antidepressants and sedatives.

I did my research on the internet and found that nursing homes use medication to alleviate pain, to treat medical conditions, and to modify behavior. According to one study, one in five patients in the nation's 15,600 nursing homes are given antipsychotic drugs that are unnecessary. One of the reasons, according to the National Center of Elder Abuse, is the staff works with a difficult population and, often, they are not well trained nor are there enough of them. They report that 50% of nursing homes are short staffed. The Center recommends more education and training for all staff especially in managing difficult resident care situations. The use of medication to modify behavior is much easier than other remedies, and there was no way I was going to be able to halt that practice. All I could do was complain periodically and suggest that they try some other strategies first. Distraction, attention, moving the resident to a different place to change the scene temporarily, soothing talk, mini massages to calm them, were all recommendations I discovered on the internet and shared with the nurses and aides. I didn't have high hopes that they would implement any of them, but I had to try. My mother was not insane, just unhappy.

I was trying everything to make her happy, but I was losing the battle. I felt hopeless and guilty that she was there. I saw no exit, no alternative placement, nothing I could do beyond what I was already doing. The same idea kept popping into my head — bring her home to live with us. Then the reality of that solution would kick in and I just kept on feeling guilty and trying to assuage my guilt with what the doctors had told me: "You'd have to turn your home into a hospital." I considered hiring an aide at least part time, but I saw what the aides did who were hired by a few families and it was not what my mother needed. They served as adjunct aides to the ones already there. The most basic tasks were managed, but the personal touch was not there. That was my daily job.

CHAPTER 21.

A Visit from Melanie

March

M elanie came to visit every few months as promised. It's a nine-hour drive from Canada, and somehow, she kept making the exhausting trip. In the spring, she came for five days because it was spring break at the college where she was a guidance counselor. I was so glad that she could take over the responsibilities with Mom for a while. She was with Mom from morning until night every day. She put her through exercises and any diversionary activities she could think of. Several times she reported that Mom seemed groggy. I was surprised because, since she'd been on different meds, she'd seemed better, at least to me.

Each evening when Mel returned from seeing Mom, we had a glass of wine together while I made dinner. I called it our Happy Hour. On the night before she was to drive home to Canada, she returned to the house and said that Mom had refused to go to dinner in the dining room, so she fed her in her room.

"That's new," I said. "She's been eating in the dining room without a problem." I was worried that this could set a bad precedent. Who would do this when Melanie was gone?

"I wouldn't want to eat in that dining room either," said Mel. "The food is unappealing and there are people in there who yell and are way below Mom cognitively. Some of the people are so impaired they're hard to look at."

I knew this, but what could I do about it? The people couldn't help how they looked and some of their behaviors did make it unpleasant to be with them, but Mom wasn't so pleasant to be with either.

"Mom's not making progress. It's been a while and she's just not moving forward. It seems like she's regressing. She should be in the higher level dining room with the more cognitively advanced people." Mel sipped some more wine and looked at me with concern.

"I have noticed that, but they're doing everything they can. It's sad and frustrating for all of us. As far as the other dining room is concerned, she's not considered independent enough. It's not so much about cognition although that is a factor that sometimes contributes to the ability to eat independently"

"Maybe Mom needs something different. Maybe some non-traditional therapies like acupuncture."

"Acupuncture?" I couldn't refrain from sounding skeptical. I wanted to be openminded but....

"Or maybe some of the newer cognitive behavior therapies. Or chiropractors?" Mel continued.

My sister has always been a believer in non-traditional medicine. I had read up on stroke victims and had not read anything about using any of those techniques with them. I hated to be a wet blanket, but I didn't hold out any hope for their efficacy. If they worked, wouldn't they appear somewhere in the literature on treatment for stroke victims?

"Mel. Those types of therapies are not covered by Medicare or her supplemental insurance. And I've never heard of them being used to treat stroke patients. If she were to get any of those treatments, she'd have to pay for them herself out of her savings. You know we have to watch her savings very carefully to cover her nursing home bills and anything else that may come up. And, I'd have to transport her to the appointments. Not a simple thing, as you know, especially since I work."

Mel accepted this in her usual calm, non-committal manner and then branched out into more idea territory. "Perhaps a paid companion would be helpful to stimulate Mom more."

"A paid companion would not offer what I do on a five day a week basis. Few people have them and from what I've seen, they're unreliable and largely unstimulating. No one keeps tabs on them. Sometimes I see them ignoring their charges. Besides, it's very expensive to have a private aide in addition to the cost of the nursing home."

Then she questioned the medications and I told her she could look at the list anytime and call the doctor to discuss. I explained that I'd done this and had come to accept that Mom needed some meds to control her anxiety. She went on to stress that "Mom needs to be with normal people as much as possible." Of course, I agreed with her. I was a strong advocate of The Inclusion Movement when I was working in the schools, and I know the benefits of people with disabilities being with people who are not disabled. But how could I make that happen? I thought it was important for Mom to be with non-disabled people, but I had no way to integrate her with the general public except for outings. Taking her out on my own was difficult and half the time, she wanted to go back to Pleasant Gardens claiming she was too tired. I had continuous pain in my back from lifting her in and out of her wheelchair and I was afraid that I'd rupture a disc at some point.

The more we talked, the more I felt unappreciated and over-whelmed. Anger began rising in my chest like a slowly simmering liquid destined to boil over. I put down my glass of wine and said, "I don't think you realize how much effort it is to take care of Mom and how difficult she can be. I have enough to do without adding to my responsibilities."

Mel said calmly, "Well, I'm just suggesting that some of the newer therapies might help her. Nothing seems to be working now."

"I know, but I can't do anymore. I just can't. The complications of setting up appointments and getting Mom there — you just don't know how hard all this is. While you're up in Canada, I'm down here dealing with it all; the bills, the calls from the nursing home, watch-ing over her care, her meds, and most of all, trying, unsuccessfully, to make her happy." At this point I was raising my voice and getting emotional.

"I just want her to get better." Melanie said, eyes reddening.

"So do I, but she's not getting better! With everything that's been done for her, she's getting worse. For now, I'm focused on mak-ing her happy, just a little bit if I can. It kills me to see her so unhappy knowing I can't change things. I just want her to be happy!" I said in a loud, tremulous voice.

"So do I," echoed Mel.

Tears were streaming down our faces now. It was the least happy Happy Hour I've ever experienced, but finally we were letting out all the pent-up feelings and thoughts we'd been avoiding for months.

I felt bad for my sister. I knew she was only trying to help and doing it from a distance had to be frustrating, but I felt relieved that I had finally let her know the toll our mother's invalidism was tak-ing on me. In keeping with our longstanding emotional distance, we didn't hug; but we understood each other. I said I'd investigate some of the therapies she suggested; she said she'd try to come down more frequently or for longer periods. We had crossed the wide no-man's land between us and met somewhere in the middle. The exchange made me realize that she was suffering, too, and being so far away, she wanted to feel like she was contributing to our mother's care.

In my heart, I knew Mom would have preferred Melanie to be the primary caregiver — she really always did like her best. We all three knew it and Mel would sometimes kid around saying, "You know Mom likes me best." I'd laugh because it was true and completely understandable. If my mother was in the room, she'd laugh, too. She didn't deny it. I was a fighter and broke down barriers letting Mel glide through adolescence without much to rebel about. I can still visualize the yelling matches between Mom and me with Mel standing off quietly to one side, an inscrutable bystander.

Now I had a chance to make things right between us. We *had* to come together for Mom's sake and for the sake of the sibling relationship that had been off the tracks for years. We shared a history that no one else did and we knew each other in a way no one else did either. Maybe this was my opportunity to try to break down the barriers between us and salvage our relationship. I'd been honest with her, and that's the first step to developing closeness. How could she know what I was going through and how I felt about it unless I told her? Well, now I had.

CHAPTER 22.

Remembering My Grandmother

To understand my relationship with my sister and my mother, you'd have to know something about how I grew up. We lived in my grandmother's big house, the one she had shared with our grandfather until he died suddenly of a heart attack at age fifty. I was a toddler when he died and have no memories of him. Shortly after his death, Mom moved in with her mother. Melanie and I were part of the package. She had recently divorced our biological father, Leo. Probably Lena thought that having her daughter around was better than being alone, at least at first, and her daughter had nowhere to go. From the beginning of our transition from Florida to this new home in New Jersey, it was clear to both Melanie and me that Lena got no joy out of having two young grandchildren living with her. I have no memory of her ever hugging or kissing me.

Lena took care of us while our mother worked at the hospital, but she was nothing like the sweet, doting, grandmother that most of my friends had. She never smiled or laughed except when she played mah-jong with her friends. She never showed us any affection. She was uninterested in our lives except when it came to enforcing rules and restrictions. She didn't allow our friends to come inside. We played outside or at friends' homes. She criticized us relentlessly and mimicked us. She seemed to enjoy making us feel worthless and annoying. For some reason, she especially picked on Melanie who reacted by trying to be invisible and stay out of her way. Gradually, my sister talked less and displayed little emotion, so I don't know what she was thinking about the situation, but I think the experience of being brought up by Lena transformed what had been a cute, funny, active little girl into a quiet, reclusive teenager. When she was ready for college, she went far away to another country — Canada. It was her escape from our dysfunctional family that she had been planning for a while.

I reacted to Lena nonconfrontationally when I was young, but later I began yelling back and arguing with her. Slapping us when we did things she didn't like was her way of saying "No!" By modern standards we were emotionally and physically abused.

In old family photos of her taken when my grandfather was still alive, I saw a woman with a slight smile who had dark red hair like my mother's and who could be considered pretty. After her husband died, her looks began to reflect her despondency. I think she was bored and lonely. She didn't drive and never tried to learn. She spent her time cleaning and cooking. Her only socialization was her mah-jong game once a week and the occasional family get-together.

I don't know if my mother knew what went on when she wasn't home, but I know it was the only way she was going to have us taken care of while she worked. The atmosphere when she was home wasn't much better. She and my grandmother argued a lot and I don't recall them showing any affection toward each either. I knew she had had a loving relationship with her father, just by the way she talked about him. I think that's where she got her softer side from.

I was a big sister bully and often fought with Melanie physically and later verbally. I regret that. I was jealous because of my mother's obvious preference for Melanie. But I also protected her and tried to help her as we were growing up. I could be mean to her, but I would not tolerate someone else mistreating her. I tried to intervene when my grandmother picked on her mercilessly, but I could only do so much. All those years of being the big sister who abused her and occasionally stood up for her took their toll on our relationship. By the time she went to college, our sibling relationship seemed irreparably damaged. Melanie had had enough and was not receptive to my occasional attempts to be close.

Lena died when we were in Junior High from a heart attack, although I heard rumors in the family that it was a suicide from an intentional overdose. Melanie and I were not sad at all and our lives, particularly Melanie's, improved after that.

CHAPTER 23

Making Time for Jack

March

I decided I had to do something with Jack that got us out of the area, away from my Mom-visits and all the distressing aspects of caregiving. I was intent on getting her better and the thought of her being alone even one day without a visit from me filled me with guilt and the fear of regression in her behavior. But I knew that for my mental health and the health of my marriage, we had to get away.

So one Sunday morning, Jack and I left town and went to the Degas exhibit at the Philadelphia museum. Sunday is the day most friends and relatives visit Pleasant Gardens, but Sunday was the day we were able to go. I knew Mom would be lonely watching the other residents with their visitors, yet I knew I had to do things with Jack. I couldn't put him in second place all the time. That was getting old, and he was not as tolerant of it as he had been initially. We weren't having much sex and I thought that a special day together would bring us closer. The truth was, I was just not interested in sex much anymore. I realized I was getting depressed by the whole situation, but I couldn't stop the downward spiral. It was like a quagmire, and I felt like I was sinking deeper and deeper into it. There was no one else to take care of her and be with her. I was mentally exhausted.

Several times I explained to Jack how torn I felt between him and my mother. I said I wanted to pay more attention to him, but it was difficult balancing his needs and hers. He was sympathetic and supportive, but he also subtly suggested that I spend less time with her and be more involved in our relationship, like I used to be. I felt like a rubber band stretched in two different directions. Both of them needed me. I couldn't even find time for myself, and the rubber band kept stretching tighter. A rubber band can break if stretched too far and I couldn't let that happen. There was a continuous video running in my head of my mother, sitting in her wheelchair, slumped over, or moaning, or staring in that strange icy way. When I went to sleep, when I woke up, whenever I drove somewhere, whenever my mind was not totally occupied with some task, the video started running.

We ate at one of the best restaurants in town and drove home feeling mellow and relaxed for the first time in a long time. It was a reconnection we both needed. We made love that night. I resolved to do things like that more often. I knew that if a marriage is going to work, you have to put effort into it and I had stopped putting in the effort. It was the second marriage for Jack and the third for me. You would think that I would have learned that trials and tribulations go along with any marriage — it's how you handle them that makes all the difference.

I knew that long after my mother was gone, Jack would be the one who would be there for me. He always had been. There never was a time when he did not support me in my aspirations or help me through my challenges. I was devoted to doing the same for him. Our marriage was a good one and we would spend the future together, I was certain. That's what I wanted, and I knew I'd better make an investment in that future.

CHAPTER 24.

After-effects of a Melanie Visit

March

As soon as I arrived at Pleasant Gardens, Mom asked why Melanie wasn't here anymore. She started moaning and crying. I explained that Mel had to go back to Canada. Mom responded with the words I was dreading. "I can't stand it here. If I have to stay here I don't want to live!" I felt like a knife had been plunged into my heart. I saw myself as the jailer holding my mother in a prison against her will. I still saw no other recourse, but I understood her emotional outburst completely. Despite the fact that I was sure I'd feel the same way, I admonished her. "Don't say that! You don't mean that!" The crying continued. "I want to go home!" she shouted at me. "If you don't stop crying and yelling, I'll leave," I said. She stopped carrying on and allowed me to wheel her into the dining room and help her eat. We were so late that there was little time for her to practice feeding herself. I hugged her and then an aide returned her to her to room.

My mind was whirring as I left the building. Where are we going Mom? This can't be life for the rest of your life. You've got to get better. Then we can move you. Please get better!

CHAPTER 25.

Accidents Will Happen?

March

Pleasant Gardens called to tell me Mom had fallen in the dining room and "took the table with her." Amazingly, she was unhurt. "How did it happen?" I asked. They explained that she was left alone in the dining room, briefly. I was furious! The person who was supposed to be watching her was giving someone else a bath. I never fully understood why she was all alone I the dining room; usually there are at least a few other people eating. Mom ate slowly as a rule, so it may be that she was the last one finished, but she should never have been left unsupervised in the dining room. She probably got tired of waiting for someone to take her back to her room and decided to try to move herself (which she has not been able to do). I pictured Mom sitting all alone in the dining room and trying to go somewhere. She must have tried to use the table to push herself away or stand up. I got to Pleasant Gardens at ten-thirty in the morning. I saw that the wheelchair was damaged in the fall and submitted a wheelchair repair request. It seemed like a detail *they* should have taken care of — it was their wheelchair.

Mom seemed okay. I asked her what happened, but she couldn't explain it. I decided we needed to practice walking with the walker again, although she had not been successful after many months. If only she could use the walker, this might not have happened. She was motivated but frustrated by the slow progress. At lunchtime she didn't like the food. I got a substitute and fed it to her. After lunch, Mom went back to her room for a nap. I went looking for the head nurse. The nurse at the main desk made a call to summon her.

The clone of Nurse Ratchet from "One Flew Over the Cuckoo's Nest" appeared with a miffed look on her face. Her platinum blonde hair was styled in a stiff page boy that looked more like a helmet than real hair. Her body had no curves. She looked like she was in an upright plank position at all times. Everything about her was severe, including her approach to her charges.

"Your mother was left alone for a very short time, and no one thought she'd have an accident sitting in her wheelchair parked at a table. She must have tried to get out of the wheelchair using the table for leverage."

"Why did the aide leave?" I asked.

"She had to leave briefly to help another resident," she said. "We don't provide one-to-one aides here."

Actually, the aide told me she had to give another person a bath, so it wasn't for a short time.

There was not an ounce of concern for my mother or me in the way the head nurse responded.

"Your mother is not adjusting well here," she added.

There was an insidious tone to her remark that made me think she might try to expel Mom, so I didn't pursue it further.

CHAPTER 26.

Feeling Helpless and Depressed

March

Depression was beginning to affect me in ways that were textbook classic. I didn't want to get out of bed. I felt tired all the time. At night, I couldn't sleep for more than two hours at a time. I couldn't stop thinking about Mom and how intolerable she found her situation. The fact that I couldn't rescue her made me feel impotent. On an intellectual level, I knew that she needed to stay where she was, but on an emotional one I couldn't accept it. I was constantly running through alternative scenarios. To take my mind off it, I forced myself to do things like go out with friends when I really had no interest in doing so. I drank extra wine at dinner. I tried to act lighthearted, but it was an effort. Sometimes I wanted to scream WHY IS GOD PUNISHING MY MOTHER?

It didn't help matters that Frisky, the cat I'd had for fifteen years, had to be put to sleep. He was Dan's pet originally and when Dan went off to college, he became mine. I'd been giving him insulin shots for his diabetes for over a year. Two times a day I would pinch the fur at the nape of his neck and insert a needle. He was completely docile and accepting of the procedure as though he knew he needed it to feel better. Then he began having chronic diarrhea and was so listless he could barely meow. Most of the time he just lay in front of the laundry room doorway where I kept his food and litter box. His name had become a pathetic misnomer; he was about as frisky as a sloth.

I took him to see our vet and he lay on the examination table as limp as a fur throw rug. Dr. Bernardo said his diabetes was out of control and he was already on an extremely high dose of insulin. He also diagnosed a heart murmur and some kind of colon problem. In short, Frisky was a mess. The doctor said I could continue treating him with more medications, and higher doses of insulin (already the highest they'd seen in a cat), but the prognosis was poor. "It might be his time, but it's your decision," said the doctor softly. I couldn't bear to see him suffer any more, so I gave the doctor the okay. He asked if I wanted to hold Frisky while he administered the needle. I couldn't do it; it would have been too hard to watch him die. I kissed him on his head several times, told him he was a good friend, and ran outside sobbing. Frisky, my furry friend for the last fifteen years was no more. It was a hard decision, but I was glad that I was able to muster up the courage to allow the doctor to put him out of his misery.

The next day, when I returned from work was the first day he didn't come trotting to the door to greet me. I felt the tremendous loss in my life. He was such a comfort to me especially with the whole Mom situation.

Euthanasia for pets in great pain or who have an extremely poor quality of life is acceptable, but humans don't have that right. Are we kinder to our pets than our loved ones? I think we are, but I dreaded ever having to make that kind of decision for Mom should it come to that.

CHAPTER 27.

Work Will Save You

March

E very day I felt like I was forcing myself to do the things I used to do automatically. I had to keep encouraging myself to continue going through my day and do the shopping, the laundry, prepare dinner, and visit Mom. The only time I didn't feel this way was when I was in front of my class, teaching and interacting with the students. When I began to speak, I became immersed in my work and thoughts of Mom evaporated. I always divided the class time between small group problem solving activities and lecture. My students gave me excellent evaluations which were important in the overall evaluation of a professor at this university. Other activities like getting grants, doing research, and serving on committees were part of my job, too, and made me focus on my other life, the one I had worked so hard to achieve, the one where I got to share all I had learned in my years of working in special education in schools at the classroom level and as an administrator. I felt I had something to give my students that would make them better teachers, beyond what was in their textbooks. There were a number of professors teaching in the same department who had never taught in a classroom and couldn't know what I had learned in the real, complex, challenging world of special education in public schools. I thought it was an important contribution I could make that might affect some of the most vulnerable, needy, and overlooked children in our schools.

The hours I spent in class working with my students made the time fly by and all my worries were left outside in the parking lot ready to be picked up when I left for home. My emotional wellbeing got a boost with every day I spent there. The preparation for each class also served as a way to focus my brain on something that did not leave room for anything but the task at hand.

Work was my savior. I didn't want to give it up.

CHAPTER 28.

A Visit from Uncle Merwin

April

t was a warm day for early April. Signs of spring were just beginning to appear; pale green buds on the trees, crocuses and lilies poking up out of the earth, red breasted robins building nests. I was happy to see my uncle, as always. He was Mom's only regular visitor besides Melanie, Jack, and me. He arrived at Pleasant Gardens in his usual jaunty good spirits and kept me laughing with his sarcastic remarks about everything from the food to the patients to the staff. His high cheek bones and tanned skin always reminded me of a Native American or maybe Paul Newman. His auburn hair had turned gray, but he was still handsome and fit from playing tennis all year long. I always referred to him as my favorite uncle and we would laugh because he was my only uncle. He loved to read mysteries, watch sports, play tennis, and discuss politics. He always said what he was thinking and there was no pretense about him. I liked that, especially now.

The softer side of Merv is one that only some people got to see. He did not engage in emotional displays of affection; he just did things that made you know he cared. He took an interest in my sister and me when we were young, and I remember that he talked to us like real people, not little children. I remember when he took us to the circus; Uncle Merwin's comments were funnier than the antics of the clowns. Whenever he came to visit, he always spent time with us. We didn't have a father in our lives at the time and I think he was trying to fill the void a little. I really got to know my uncle after Mom had the stroke. He revealed his serious side and told me how close he felt to his sister and how important it was to him to be there for her. In addition to cheering me up with his humorous commentary on Pleasant Gardens, Merv reassured me that I was doing a great job after every visit. His emotional support was a tremendous source of comfort and strength for me.

We ate lox platters in the dining room. Mom smiled weakly at him and was glad to see him but was not her usual ebullient self when her only sibling and favorite person, next to Melanie, was around. It was a beautiful day and I decided we should all get out of the melancholic atmosphere of Pleasant Gardens and go on an outing to Smithville, a colonial village with unique shops, restaurants, a lake with ducks and swans, and quaint cobblestone streets. It was the kind of place Mom had always enjoyed.

She was not impressed. She protested that the cobblestones were too bumpy for her wheelchair, and they were. We found some paved areas. I was as enthusiastic as a real estate agent trying to make a sale pointing out the ducks, the lake, the colonial reproduction buildings, the flowers, the cute shops, but she was not interested. After one hour she wanted to go back. I didn't know how many more outings I could take her on with the poor returns on my investment that I was getting.

Merwin was, as always, a fountain of praise for the care I'd been giving to his sister. He may not have lifted Mom's spirits, but he lifted mine. We left her in her room all curled up in a ball ready for a nap. In the elevator going down to the parking lot, I began to cry. I told him how guilty I felt having her in a nursing home. Merwin, never a warm fuzzy guy, patted me on the shoulder and said, "You're doing just fine. No one could do more." His words meant so much to me. Maybe he's right, I thought. Maybe no one *could* do more. He left in an uncharacteristically subdued mood to make the long drive back up north.

CHAPTER 29.

The Love Story of Tom and Doris

April

A nursing home is a different world. It's nothing like the real world outside. Everything inside is about being sick or incapacitated. It's depressing. There is nothing uplifting about being there. As one resident in her nineties said, "No one *wants* to be here. They're only here because they *have* to be." It's a life of confinement and segregation. At least if there were somewhere to go in a wheelchair; a neighborhood, a main street, a park, but there was nothing near Pleasant Gardens. The residents were effectively excluded from the real world of shops, theaters, malls, and people. Human contact was limited to visitors (if you had any), staff, and the other residents. Conversation was thus of an extremely limited variety and not very stimulating. That's why it no longer surprised me anymore that the residents didn't interact with each other, didn't laugh, didn't converse, and seemed to just exist.

The exceptions were Tom and Doris.

In the spring, young love blossoms everywhere. I never imagined that spring fever would hit Pleasant Gardens, but I was wrong. Love can grow like a flower even in the desert — unlikely but still, it happens sometimes. It happened to one man and one woman in

Pleasant Gardens. I noticed that they were always together. They sought each other out and spent their time gazing out windows together, talking, laughing, whispering, and holding hands. They parked their wheelchairs together, went up and down the halls in tandem, or just spent time smiling at each other. Tom was a good-looking man with lively blue eyes that crinkled when he smiled (which was often) and thinning white hair. Doris was attractive, too, with delicate features, pale lemony-white short hair, only slightly wrinkled skin, and a sweet facial expression. Her eyes sparkled whenever she looked into Tom's.

I thought they were married, but a staff member told me that wasn't the case. They were married, but not to each other. I also heard that the staff was supposed to start keeping them apart; they were spending too much time together and the families didn't like it. Oh yes, and there was another reason. The head staff members had observed Tom getting too physically intimate with Doris. That's what one of the aides whispered to me. What could that be I wondered? Did he kiss her, or touch her inappropriately? I never heard the details and would never ask. I just noticed that they were gradually separated more. I heard them protest and ask where the other one was. They were told the other one was busy. Very quickly the glow was gone from their faces and the light in their eyes disappeared. They began to look like everyone else on the floor; downcast and apathetic. It was one of the saddest things I have ever witnessed. Two lonely people who had found that rarity in a nursing home, a human connection, a person they looked forward to seeing each day, a reason to live, were severed from each other.

Was there another way to handle it? I guess it depended on the families of Tom and Doris to allow the relationship. The off limits type of contact could have been explained to Tom and monitored by staff. If that had happened, Tom and Doris would have been able to continue to enjoy the company of a person with whom they had developed a relationship. Friendship, attraction, or whatever you want to call it; it was a reason to get up in the morning.

Loneliness in nursing homes is a huge problem that impacts the mental health of the residents. In some nursing homes, volunteers are organized to act as friendly visitors assigned to a particular person. Another very effective antidote is pet visitors. If it is the same pet, the residents begin to look forward to visits from that dog (or cat). This is also carried out by volunteers. These efforts will alleviate boredom and provide stimulation, but they cannot meet the overall loneliness crisis that afflicts nursing homes.

What can? According to my research, friendly visitors have the most impact, but some nursing homes do not allow them. Senior residential centers that are set in a community where the residents have access to that community and have regular interaction with members of the community make them feel included in society. This is the kind of thinking that inspired the creation of group homes for people with cognitive delays and other disabilities rather than large institutional settings years ago. Even small communities set up within a large institution can be nurtured where residents share small spaces within the larger buildings. The members of these smaller communities interact with each other and become like families. Like a suite, several rooms share a sitting area and have access to game tables with puzzles, cards, and reading natter,. The same nurse's aide interacts with them each day. Companionship occurs more easily because of the smaller setting. Nurturing togetherness is a staff member's job.

I learned about these new philosophies regarding nursing homes on the internet and wished I could have found one that put these ideas into practice. I am certain Mom would have adjusted better to her new living arrangement if Pleasant Gardens had implemented any of these ideas. As it was, she was lost in the large group she found herself in, and I was losing her.

CHAPTER 30.

The Going Home Experiment

April

Somewhere I read that the three plagues of nursing homes are boredom, loneliness, and helplessness. These comprised the everyday experience of my mother. I was no match for them, and I couldn't combat them very effectively with my daily visits. Then a new plague beset my mother's floor — Yelling Man. He sat in his wheelchair near the nurses' station, yelled continuously, and banged on the wall when he could reach it. His refrain was the same, over and over again: "Get me out of here! Take me home! Someone help me." It was pathetic. He was probably a little out of his mind and was simultaneously driving everyone else out of theirs'. Yelling Man could be heard up and down all the hallways leading to the nurses' station. After three days of this, I asked one of the nurses what could be done about it and she said, "Nothing. He has a right to be here. Some people take time to adjust." "But what about everyone else's right to a peaceful existence?" I asked. She answered cautiously, "He may have to be moved eventually if his meds don't start working."

Mom had a pained expression on her face when I found her parked outside the door to her room. "Do you want to go somewhere?" I asked her. "Yes please, anywhere," she said. I took her to a small strip mall nearby for a manicure which she enjoyed. Afterwards, I decided to take her to my house rather than back to the torture of Yelling Man, at least for a while. It was a dream I had nurtured for quite a while — bring Mom home for a visit. I imagined how I'd watch her face light up as she realized where she was. Then I'd wheel her around the first floor of the house where she spent a couple of weeks every summer. I was giddy with anticipation at how delighted she'd be to be in familiar surroundings where she had spent so many happy times with Jack and Dan and me. It was to be a test situation to observe her reaction and, if positive, I would gradually lengthen the visits working up to weekends spent with us.

When we pulled up to the house, I asked her if she knew where we were. "Of course," she said. That didn't necessarily mean anything though. She answered questions that way frequently. I got her out of the car and into the wheelchair, then out of the wheelchair and half carried her and helped her walk up the three steps to the front door. I got her into the hallway, and she couldn't make it any farther, so I let her sit on the floor while I got the wheelchair into the house. It took several attempts to get her back in the wheelchair and my back was killing me. I rolled her around the first floor. She didn't react any differently from wheeling her around anywhere else. I had expected her to be so excited to be in my home again for the first time since her stroke. She began slumping in the chair and making her noises. As soon as I lifted her up under her arms into a sitting position, she slid back down again. The doctor said that the slumping was an involuntary neurological activity. I decided she'd be more comfortable on the couch and at least wouldn't be slumping anymore. I made a lounge chair out of the couch with pillows. Now she was safe. She kept making those noises like grunts or chanting: "Unhh! Unhh!" which also seemed involuntary. She was not in pain, but she was not happy.

I made her a tuna fish sandwich and fed it to her on the sofa. When she was finished, I got her back in the wheelchair and wheeled her into the den where the computer was. She used to love to send e-mails back and forth with her friends. Mostly they exchanged jokes. I asked if she wanted to send mail to anyone. She looked at me blankly and began rocking and chanting again. I suggested returning to Pleasant Gardens and she didn't balk one bit.

What I learned: she behaved no differently in my house than at the facility. What this meant: if she lived with me her behavior might be the same.

Good news awaited me at work. After months of worrying whether I would be able to stay on at the college, my colleagues told me I was in for another year. The department applied for a "line" and got it. They said I'd have to meet with the search committee as a standard procedure, but my professor friends were sure I would get it. My evaluations in all my classes were outstanding. So, one worry would be out of the way as soon as I got the contract and signed it.

I thanked each class for their support and told them this was proof of their power. A few months back, when they heard that I might not be returning next year, one of them wrote a petition and all my classes signed it, insisting that the department find a way to keep me on. When I shared the good news in each of my classes, they applauded. I wanted to keep my job for many reasons; a sense of pride in my work, a belief that I was doing something that mattered by training teachers to work with students with special needs, a desire to contribute to the family income, but the most important one had become, an escape from my homelife into a completely different world.

CHAPTER 31.

The Feeding Tube War

April

When Mom had the stroke back in September, the doctors inserted a feeding tube in her stomach and provided nutrition through this method. A feeding tube is a plastic tube with a stopper on the end of it that dangles from a person's stomach over their clothing. It is visible and so is the stuff that regurgitates into it at times. It must be flushed several times a day to be kept sanitary. It looks like a transparent plastic tail hanging out of the front of a person's body. Sometimes the cork popped, and it spurted foul smelling digested food all over my mother's clothes. It was disgusting and just one more indignity Gertrude had to endure. When she was eating on her own they kept the feeding tube in place in case there was any further need for it. It was understandable up to a point. After she was eating for a few months I asked that the tube be removed since it wasn't being used and maybe never would be again. Pleasant Gardens refused. That's when the Feeding Tube War began.

The nursing home director told me the doctors who put it in were the only ones who could recommend that it be removed. That was impossible since the team that worked on her was up in Elizabeth. I didn't even know who they were. So, I contacted the doctor we'd been using since coming down to south Jersey and asked if he could take it out. He said that was up to the nursing home, not him. Back I went to the head nurse and asked her why my mother still had a plastic feeding tube hanging out of her body after eight months. The head nurse clone of Nurse Ratchet fixed me with her glacier-blue eyes and said, "Your mother may need that feeding tube someday. Do you want her to die?"

Not a good way to start a dialogue, I thought. "Of course, I don't want her to die. If she ever needs it, I'm sure it can be implanted. So far, she hasn't needed it in months. Is this a forever thing? I'd like to take her places and have her stay over-night some day without worrying about flushing the tube."

"I'm sorry to tell you that at your mother's age there are many situations that require the use of a feeding tube and it's certainly easier for everyone if it's already in place. If your mother starts losing weight or shows a drop in her calcium levels, we need to use the feeding tube."

So, I guess it was about convenience for them. I went back to her treating doctor who is also a staff doctor with Pleasant Gardens and repeated these arguments for keeping a feeding tube in place indefinitely. I told him I did not think the *possibility* of a problem was enough of a reason to keep the feeding tube in place forever when there had been no history of a problem since her stroke. He advised me to talk to the staff nutritionist and see what he thought. Now it seemed like everyone was shifting responsibility.

I had just finished feeding Mom her lunch one Saturday afternoon when Bob, the nutritionist approached and asked to speak to me. A sandy haired young man with a perennially phony smile, Bob looked anorexic. He took me aside and spoke in hushed, serious tones while reviewing my mother's chart.

"Your mother has been losing weight."

"How much?"

"About five pounds so far."

"What does it mean?" I asked fearfully, thinking cancer.

"She's not eating enough."

"But she eats her entire meal whenever I'm here."

Bob cocked his head, smiled wistfully, and said, "If only you could always be here."

"What are you saying? That other people are not feeding her?"

He ignored the question.

"I can add supplemental milkshakes to her diet, but if that doesn't work we'll have to go to the feeding tube."

"I am absolutely opposed to the feeding tube being used in this way. Get more staff and feed her! She can't feed herself adequately." My voice was rising.

Bob began to turn away, carefully showing no emotion.

"Listen, I don't want my mother fed through a tube. She needs to be in the dining room with other people eating like a normal human being!"

Skinny Bob was slowly heading down the hall.

"Maybe you're the one who should be on a feeding tube," I yelled after him.

Something did not seem right here. I did a little research on-line and found that many agencies, doctors, and researchers find the use of feeding tubes worrisome. The tube may be used to feed patients when there is not enough staff to manage the job. It may be associated with increased risk of infection and discomfort. One study said that Medicaid unintentionally provides a fiscal incentive by paying more for patients on tubes. For the profit motivated nursing homes, hand feeding means adding employees thus increasing costs. Another problem is that confused patients sometimes yank the tubes out. The best news was a list of alternatives to tube feeding enumerated on different websites including prompting the resident to eat, feeding by hand, providing therapy to improve swallowing skills, and providing assistive devices for eating. The Nursing Home Reform Act states that slow eating is not a reason for inserting a tube nor is shortage of staff. Mealtimes can be staggered if staff is in short supply. It further states handfeeding is preferred for medical and emotional reasons and a resident who has been able to eat on their own or with assistance should not be fed through a tube unless a clinical condition is present which demonstrates a tube is unavoidable.

I had not thought about the psychological benefits of hand feeding before, but it makes sense. For residents where the outside world and their world are bifurcated, and loneliness is a chronic problem, hand feeding provides human contact. I should have realized this because that is what I'd been doing with my mother all these months although I was focused on the nutritional benefits.

Armed with all this information I met with the nutritionist again. He was unmoved. I persisted, "Maybe it has something to do with whether she likes the meals that day, or, more likely, it has something to do with the people responsible for feeding her. Do they give her the assistance she needs? Do they encourage her?"

"They do their job. Your mother has lost weight and so the tube must stay in place in case we need to use it." He flashed his smile again like a light that he turned on and then flicked off and began walking purposefully down the hall. I was furious. Did he have complete control over this matter? What about the consumer? What about the family?

I Lose the Feeding Tube War

April

I arrived to give Mom dinner and found her hooked up to the god-
damn feeding tube! She was staring up at the ceiling while dinner
flowed into her stomach through the IV. In the twilight with no
lights on, the scene made me think of a prisoner being subjected to
a procedure they have no control over. I just froze and then quickly
backed away from the door. I didn't want her to see me. It was too
sad, and I had no answers for her.

Out in the hall an aide told me it was started yesterday, ordered
by that sneaky nutritionist, Skinny Bob. How did he do that after our
conversation? I was so sick of being ignored and controlled by the
place I was paying to take care of my mother. Did they think I should
have no say in her care? I was her guardian. The doctors wouldn't
remove the tube because the nursing home insisted it was necessary. They said they depended on the nutritionist's assessment. Even
the slightest drop in weight was cause for alarm. Records on weight
loss are one of the things that monitors look at when they check
nursing homes along with documentation of bed sores and falls and
other possible signs of neglect. I understood that weight loss should
be monitored but the real question was why was she losing weight?

From my observations in the dining room it could be that no one helped her eat. She needed assistance and encouragement and I don't think she was getting either because she was somewhat able to feed herself, but very slowly. There were people there who needed hand-feeding on a constant basis, and they were the only ones getting the attention from the limited staff in the dining room. I set out to find the nutritionist. I was angry and ineffably sad. Was this her fate to be at the mercy of the nutritionist who has no control over the staffing necessary to make sure everyone eats their meals?

The nutritionist was not around at night, so I had to wait to track him down the next day.

We had our discussion in the hallway as usual; I don't know if he had an office, but he never suggested meeting there so our conversations were out in the open., completely lacking in privacy.

"Why did you start the feeding tube?" I asked.

Skinny Bob gave me his fake smile and said," Because your mother has lost weight and needs to gain it back. It's right there in her chart. She's lost five pounds. We don't want to let the situation continue."

"Why didn't you try supplements first?"

"We didn't want to wait too long. Sometimes that takes a long time to get the desired effect."

I had seen those little cans of Boost sitting next to residents, opened, and not being consumed. Nobody made sure the people drank them; they just made sure that they were provided. I encountered this situation with my mother when I arrived in the late afternoon a couple of times. There she sat; an opened can of Boost on a table next to her wheelchair. She hadn't drunk a drop.

There was no doubt I was being given the runaround and they had no intention of ever removing the feeding tube. I'm sure they were playing it safe and keeping the tube ever ready to keep my mother fed one way or another. Investing in more staff was not part of their plan. I decided to look around for another nursing home. Someone had told me that the county home was a really good alternative. The connotation of 'county home' did not sound appealing to me, but I had to give it a try.

CHAPTER 33.

The Last Straw

April

We went on a vacation with another couple to Mohonk Mountain in New York. I wanted to spend time with Jack away from the day-to-day of Mom, work, and the despair that was overtaking me regarding Mom's situation. I paid one of the aides to be with Mom every day on her days off while I was away so Mom wouldn't be unattended or lonely. Three days went by quickly and I did not think of Mom very much. I believed she'd be safe; Pleasant Gardens had my number if they needed me, and I was only hours away. We spent our time playing golf, paddle boating, hiking, and just sitting on the wraparound veranda rocking in the Adirondack chairs. Beautiful green mountains surround the resort, everything is so secluded. The mountain air was crisp and cool, as refreshing as an ice cream cone on a summer day. Cares were far away.

When I got back home, Mom stared at me with the eyes of a zombie. She showed no sign of recognition. She looked at me hard as though trying to place me. After I sat with her at lunch and she never uttered a word, I sent her off to her room for a nap with an aide and went in search of the nurse.

"What happened to my mother? She's totally different than when I left."

The nurse was a substitute nurse for the usual one in charge who had gone on vacation. She was young and seemed flustered.

"I don't know your mother very well, so I haven't noticed the changes you see. We can look at her chart and see what's been happening the past few days."

She gave me the chart and I immediately noticed that the medications were not the ones Dr. Gelb had ordered.

"These are meds her doctor took her off months ago. Why is she back on them?"

The young nurse seemed extremely nervous and asked if I wanted to talk with the director of the nursing home. I said I did and marched down to his office. His secretary said I would have to make an appointment. My appointment was the next day.

I met with Mr. Chandler in his office in the administration wing on the main floor. He sat at one end of a highly polished conference table near his desk while the young substitute nurse sat opposite me. The office was beautifully decorated in an up-to-date color palette of burnt orange and beige with dark mahogany furniture. It looked expensive. Len, as he liked to be called by community members who support Pleasant Gardens, stood, and greeted me with a big smile and a firm handshake. He was someone I was familiar with mainly from fundraising activities for the facility. Before Mom became a resident, Jack and I were steadfast supporters of Pleasant Gardens and attended the large annual dinner dance fundraiser every year. I always thought it was a worthy cause. That was before I got an inside look.

I had never seen Len on the residents' floors. A middle aged, slightly pudgy man with black shiny hair that looked like patent leather, he folded his hands on the table, beamed his friendly smile filled with amazingly white teeth at me, and said, "So, I hear you're concerned about the meds your mother has been getting." "Yes," I said. "I am very concerned because they are not correct. That could be a recipe for disaster," I continued. Len kept smiling as though this was no big deal and said, "Jennifer here is substituting for the head nurse who is on vacation, and she may not have been aware of the changes to your Mom's medications." I persisted saying that she should have been, and getting the right medications was one of the most important parts of a patient's care, wouldn't he agree? His smile was still beaming, but a little less brilliantly. "Of course, it is. I totally agree. I assure you that this will be rectified and never happen again. Jennifer wants to apologize to you." Poor Jennifer looked like a scolded yet contrite child and said she was sorry and added that she was new and didn't always do things right. I smiled at her as nicely as I could considering she could kill someone. Was she at fault or was her superior who was away and in charge of the chart? Was she being made a scapegoat? I turned back to Len.

"This could have been a tragic mistake with severe ramifications. I don't think an apology is going to help. I think Jennifer was following what was on the chart, which is not something she has control over. I now feel as though I will have to check the chart on a regular basis to see if the correct medications are being given. This is not the only problem I have observed involving medications. On two occasions I saw an aide about to give my mother certain pills that were supposed to be crushed and they weren't. I asked her to check the chart and note that those pills needed to be crushed, which she did, but what if I had not been there? Would my mother have choked?" I tried to remain calm, but I could hear indignation creeping into my voice.

Len's pudgy fingers wrapped and unwrapped around each other like fat larvae. "I'm sorry that happened, but I knew nothing about it until this moment. I'll make sure all aspects of your mother's meds are monitored carefully."

"But, Len, shouldn't your staff have been doing that all along?"

Len was no longer smiling. "Bethanie, I don't think we're making much headway here. If you would like to take this matter further, arbitration is a path you can pursue."

Obviously, he didn't think I would make trouble for him since my mother was still there. I remembered that there was a clause about arbitration in the contract I signed with Pleasant Gardens and vowed to look it up when I got home. Len stood abruptly, signaling the meeting was over.

There was something wrong with this whole picture. I didn't feel like fighting. I felt like getting my mother out and finding someplace where she would be safer.

What really incensed me was that my mother was not a Medicaid patient getting all her nursing home costs covered. She wasn't income eligible for it, and so Medicare paid some of the bills but all the rest came out of her bank account. She was a paying consumer of a service that didn't seem to care about her as long as she kept on paying the bills. At least they could provide the services we were paying for. A change was on the way as soon as I could make it happen. I was done with this rip-off.

CHAPTER 34

A New Residence for Mom

April

I visited the Bayview nursing home and applied for Mom's admission. The facility passed state inspection with high marks. This time I knew to look on-line at Medicare.gov. and knew what to look for. The Nursing Home Reform Act requires states to conduct unannounced surveys, including resident interviews, at least once every fifteen months. The Medicare website lists the most recent federal survey results and facts about nursing home ownership. Bayview seemed to have a lot more staff and definitely more RNs. It's a county facility as opposed to a private one. Although it is not as pretty and is much older, the staff seemed to me, during my tour, to have a more compassionate, interested attitude and there seemed to be more people around to care for my mother. Everywhere I looked staff members were scurrying about. I had heard the pay is slightly higher at a state-run facility and the benefits are better.

I notified Pleasant Gardens that my mother was moving to another facility and instructed them to send her records over there. I didn't tell my mother details of when and where this would happen so as not to have her worry about it. On the appointed morning I arrived in her room and started packing up her stuff. She was dressed and ready to go. I got her into my own collapsible wheelchair and headed down the hall as fast as possible not making eye contact with anyone. I felt like we were breaking out of prison, and I didn't want to stop and chat or say goodbye to anyone. The director was standing in the reception area on the first floor outside his office glaring at me. I know he was glad to see us go despite losing a lucrative non-Medicaid patient.

"Bethanie where are we going?" asked Mom.

"We're going to a new place for you, it's much better than this one. I think you'll like the change of scenery." I wheeled her down the corridor like I was driving a get-away car and had to make our escape. As we cleared the front door I felt a tremendous rush of relief and optimism.

We arrived at Bayview Residence and were warmly greeted by the staff who helped us get her room organized. Mom was in a good mood and seemed to like the new room and all the friendly staff members who introduced themselves. Bayview was not nearly as posh as Pleasant Gardens but there was energy in the atmosphere that was contagious. People, both residents and staff, were in evidence everywhere. She ate one hundred percent of her lunch and the dietician said, "Let's not do tube feeding. Let's use Ensure plus meds to see if her weight can be maintained." I didn't even suggest it! That first day, they figured out that a wheelchair with a pommel would work to keep her from sliding forward and give her more stability. They placed mats around the bed at night to protect her if she fell. They gave her a bed with short bedrails. Lower bedrails are better, they said, because patients will climb over if they really want to no matter how high the rails are and the fall will be worse. In short, they met problems with solutions on our first day. I was filled with wonder and gratitude. Why hadn't I looked for a different place for her to live sooner? I castigated myself, knowing the answer was, I didn't know any place else could be different. I was an uneducated consumer.

Mom made the transition easily. She seemed energized by the change. She knew it was a new setting, but since it was still a nursing home, she didn't react much at all. Although she didn't say it, I think she understood I had made the change because I wanted something better for her. She was always happy to see me and didn't complain as much about not being home. She was still making her little noises and rocking some but I felt maybe we had turned a corner. Was it possible she was adjusting? I hoped so.

The décor is more institutional, and the layout is immense, but Mom didn't seem to care. Her room was smaller, but it was set up basically the same way as Pleasant Gardens and everyone had a roommate. In a county run facility, they don't have money to invest in making it beautiful. No aviaries or murals in the lobby and the rooms are not as modern. Instead, they keep everything scrupulously clean and hire more staff. I asked the head nurse, Lottie, about the reason for the difference and she said the county facilities are more accountable than private nursing homes. They must meet strict standards and submit to more frequent inspections. Lottie was always out on the floor checking on things. She was lean, flat chested, wore her reddish hair in a crew cut, and exuded efficiency mixed amply with compassion. Lottie had had a double mastectomy and was only recently back on the job. I quickly felt I could talk to her about anything, and she would have time for my concerns. That feeling proved to be accurate. What a change from Nurse Ratchet!

One day, after Mom's feeding tube spurted smelly vomit-like liquid all over her pants after lunch, I asked Lottie about feeding tubes and the possibility of removing Mom's. Her response was to guide me to a hallway I had never been on. The rooms were dimly lit and each person in them was hooked up to a bag of liquid hanging next to their bed. "These people are all on feeding tubes. They may never get off them. Some are unconscious. They need to be here to stay alive. Your mother doesn't need a feeding tube. She's gaining weight through other methods. I'll broach the subject with the powers that be, and we'll have a meeting. You'll attend." I left that dismal hallway and the people who looked catatonic with a feeling of trepidation about what could happen to Gertrude if she ever needed the feeding tube long-term, concomitant with a feeling of renewed hope that the tube would be removed at last.

CHAPTER 35

It's Better at Bayview

April

Mom was doing better at Bayview. She had not lost any weight since her arrival. She wasn't talking much but smiled when I arrived and kissed me each time. She was back in physical therapy because she'd shown improvement. They had her getting up and walking while holding on to their hands every two hours. I tried it and she was walking better but still couldn't walk independently at all. The activities for the residents were much the same as those in Pleasant Gardens and Mom had little interest in them, but she got much more attention from the staff. They were less business-like and probably had had better training on how to interact with the residents warmly and patiently. The difference was immense!

The staff social worker, Teresa, quickly became involved with Mom and established a relationship with her. She was a heavy-set middle-aged woman with big dimples that made her appear to be perpetually smiling and she did seem to be in a constant happy state of mind. She always wore cheery colors and novelty earrings that added to the upbeat impression she gave. She had succeeded in getting Mom involved in some activities. When they showed movies, Mom stayed in the community room to watch. When they had manicure parties, Mom was happy to have her nails done with a group of women, talking to the volunteer manicurist, and interacting with some of the residents. Teresa was always available to talk with me if I wanted to discuss Mom's progress. The staff made sure Mom was seated with other residents and was not alone in the corridor as she sometimes was at Pleasant Gardens. Usually the residents clustered near the nurse's station or in front of the TV, but the staff let Mom stay in her bed in the afternoons if she felt like it. She liked to watch some TV but didn't feel the need to do it in a group. I was so relieved that the staff was incredibly involved in all aspects of her care, and they were developing personal relationships with her.

The administration was so much more flexible. They realized quickly that my mother was stubborn and could cause a ruckus if forced to do things she didn't want to do. They allowed her to keep her light on and read as long as she wanted to after dinner perusing some books with pictures like travel guides (even thought she could no longer read them) and magazines until she fell asleep. She had always read in bed before going to sleep for as long as I could remember.

Nursing homes are very concerned about preventing bed sores, infections, weight loss, poor hygiene, and that's how they are rated, but they have failed to consider the person's happiness and concomitantly, their independence. Bayview took the psychological well-being of their residents very seriously. They individualized their care plans. Not everyone is the same and personal preferences were considered in the management of their care to a much greater extent than Pleasant Gardens. Finally we were in a place that was patient centered, a place that wanted the residents to be healthy *and* happy.

CHAPTER 36.

Cats, Dogs, and Butterflies

April

One of the best things about Bayview is its location — it's in a neighborhood. When I took Mom outside for a walk we saw houses, flowers, people, birds, babies, animals, in other words — life. There was a wide bike path right across the street from Bayview. Bike riders, babies in carriages and strollers, people walking their dogs, kids on skateboards, passed by us. Squirrels leaping about in the grass and scampering up tree trunks delighted us. People tending their gardens, raking leaves, playing ball, depending on the season, provided activities for us to observe. Everywhere, even on cold days, people were out walking or jogging. We encountered nature and humanity; things sorely lacking in the isolated area where Pleasant Gardens was located. These excursions lifted both our spirits.

It was a lovely, warm day in April, when we went for one of our usual walks on the bike path. We talked to people about their dogs, and they stopped to let us pet them. The dogs were just as friendly to Mom as they were to anyone who was not in a wheelchair. Her face lit up every time we got someone to stop and let us interact with their dog. It was a part of life she missed. Once we met a lady with a cat on a leash. We were astounded that the cat didn't mind the leash.

We stopped to talk to the woman. She was very friendly and said she had trained her cat to walk on a leash so she could walk on the bike path, but it caused too much of a stir among the many dogs. So now she just walked the cat in front of her house. Mom said to me when we left, "That cat reminds me of Frisky. So fat."

Some nursing homes have pet therapy dogs who visit the patients. Some go farther and keep pets on the premises where residents enjoy their non-judgmental, ever affectionate, joyful presences. The staff takes care of them, and they add a special warmth to life in the nursing home. Other nursing homes have installed a parakeet in each resident's room (if they want one) and the brightly colored living presence creates a connection with the outside world.

In other nursing homes, house plants are provided and tended in every room. I bought a plant for Mom's room, a hardy succulent jade plant that I took care of when I visited. Mom, who loved house plants and her garden, enjoyed having it there even though she couldn't personally care for it. She'd remind me to water it and would pinch the leaves sometimes to check its health. That jade plant was thriving. They say plants feel vibes from people and need love along with the water and fertilizers. If that's true, Mom was providing the love.

After walking for a while, we stopped to rest at one of the many benches along the bike path, each one with a metal plate stating who it is dedicated to. The sun felt good. I tilted my face up to absorb the warmth. I could smell the honey-suckle nearby. A small plain white butterfly was flitting about near us. Mom pointed to it and said, "I think that's Barbara."

"Barbara?" I asked.

"Yes, Cousin Barbara. She's come to visit me."

Barbara was one of my mother's favorite cousins. She died many years before Mom's stroke. I remember her being very upset about it at the time.

"I feel so sad for her; that she's not here anymore to enjoy all the trees and the beautiful flowers," she said in a wistful voice. "But maybe she's here now."

It was more sentences than I'd heard her say in a long time. I wondered if she had been holding out on me until she thought she had to express herself.

"Maybe she is," I agreed. I have friends who believe that a dearly departed relative or friend visited them in some form or another and it made them happy. There seemed to be no harm in allowing Mom this comforting thought.

The white butterfly hung around us for a longer time than I would expect for a butterfly, then fluttered delicately away.

CHAPTER 37.

Mother's Day Brunch

May

Melanie arrived late at night after her long drive from Canada. The next morning, we picked up Mom and took her out for a Mother's Day Brunch. The restaurant was crowded. We maneuvered her wheelchair into place at a table and I hoped she wouldn't have a meltdown which was common for her in restaurants. She didn't. She was perfectly behaved. She ate her waffles with fresh fruit and raved about each piece of fruit saying how much she missed it. Odd, because she was never much of a fruit eater. Melanie and I presented her with a few little Mother's Day presents that she could use at Bayview; a classical CD for her portable CD player, a few pairs of socks with pictures of animals on them like she loved, and some moisturizing cream with a gardenia scent (her favorite flower.) She was happy with everything.

When we got her back to her room, I looked around for the portable CD player and it was nowhere in sight. I reported it to the nurse on duty. Theft by wandering residents was usually the reason something went missing. I propped up her Mother's Day cards on her bureau, so she could enjoy them some more and so that everyone who came in her room would know that she had children who cared.

I recalled the prescient card I had sent her one year ago which said, 'I want to repay you for all your hard work; when you get senile I promise to make sure your socks always match.' Those were the days when we could joke about such things.

Someone showed up with the missing CD player. They had found it in someone else's room. Mom got back in her bed saying she was tired. When I suggested TV she said, "I've had enough of that for a year." I watered the jade plant, put some classical music on her CD player and snuck out as she dozed off.

There is only one reason I like classical music today — Mom used to play it in the house on a record player she bought with Green Stamps. She bought a set of albums, maroon-colored like a set of encyclopedias, that contained all the great classical composers and their music. She encouraged Melanie and me to think about what the music sounded like or what it reminded us of; a stampede of horses, a sunset, a troop of soldiers, a rainstorm, fairies flitting about an enchanted garden? I still visualize things when I listen to classical music. Music appreciation is one of the great gifts she gave me.

Mother's Day was a success! No outbursts, no rocking and chanting, and no crying. Melanie remarked, "Mom is improving." Maybe she is, only time will tell, I thought. Melanie and I watched TV late into the night. We discussed the state of Mom's finances but not Mom. Right after an early breakfast, Mel headed back to Canada. I don't know how she kept on making that long arduous trip, but I was glad she did. Mom needed to see her, and I needed to feel less alone in this.

CHAPTER 38.

The Feeding Tube is History

Late May

At the last care plan meeting, I talked with Lottie, the nutritionist, Theresa, and the recreation therapist about removing the feeding tube. Theresa was strong in her approval. She had gotten to know Mom and me well. The nutritionist expressed concern that "someday, she might need it." I responded, "Does that mean that for the next who knows how many years my mother has to have a plastic tube dangling from her body? I want her to come home and stay with me on weekends and it is an impediment to that goal with all the flushing requirements and fear of it coming out." Lottie acknowledged that the tube can be intimidating and added that Mom's weight had been stable. They all agreed to take it up with the presiding doctor.

The next time I visited, there was only a surgical dressing where the tube had been. Hallelujah! They also started a new medication, which seemed to be working — less crying. She was mellower but not fully 'there.' I guessed this was a medication tradeoff.

CHAPTER 39.

Feeding Time at the Zoo

June

B ayview was a big improvement over Pleasant Gardens but making sure my mother ate enough food was still a concern. I was
often there at dinner time after work. There were about ten tables
in the dining room on her floor with six people to a table, every one
of them in a wheelchair. It was called the communal dining room but
little communing took place among the residents.

During a typical dinner time meal, I would sit next to Mom
and try to get her to eat a little bit of each menu item. All around
us people would sit staring at their food instead of eating it. Others
tried to eat and were unsuccessful. They couldn't keep the food on
the utensil, or they couldn't get it on the utensil in the first place.
Food would be dropping everywhere, on the floor, in their laps, and
back onto their plates. As frustrating as it was for them, none complained. They knew they had to do the best they could before the
dinner hour was over. The only ones who got assistance eating were
the ones the staff referred to as The Feeders. They were the residents
who could not possibly feed themselves. Even though Mom could
barely use her left non-dominant arm and had no use of her right

arm, she was not considered a Feeder. I was afraid she might starve if I didn't show up for at least one meal.

On one particular evening we were seated with Roberta, who tried again and again to lift a cup of juice to her lips, but her hand trembled so much that the juice just flew around in space landing mostly on the table and her. Everyone wore bibs, but still things were a mess. The Blind Lady tried to eat, too, but had no idea where anything was and ended up eating air off her fork as often as food. Then there was the Dog Lady, who ate by putting her face into her plate like someone's pet puppy. If you put a utensil in her hand, she'd use it for a few bites and then resume her dog imitation. Incredibly, these people were not considered Feeders because they *could* eat somewhat independently. The line had to be drawn because there were not enough aides to assist everyone who needed assistance. I tried to help some of the people sitting at our table, but I couldn't do much for them because Mom needed me for every bite. The whole scene was bizarre and pathetic.

Dessert that night was mud-colored pudding. Mom was not enthralled. People sitting at our table were having cake, my mother's favorite dessert.

"Beth, I think I'd like some cake tonight," she said in a calm voice as though it were just an ordinary request and did not completely override her dietary restrictions.

"Oh, if only you could," I said as sympathetically as possible, "but you see they didn't give you cake. They gave you something that looks like crème Brule." Mom was not swayed.

"Beth, I'm really tired of that gooey stuff, and I want cake," she said giving me her stern mother look. Suddenly I was no longer feeding my mother her meal — I was the daughter being told what to do.

"But you could choke on the crumbs," I reminded her.

"I don't give a crap! I want a piece of cake!" She yelled. She was starting to have a meltdown.

"Okay, okay," I said as I stole The Blind Lady's piece of cake off her tray. Yes, I had been reduced to stealing from the blind. I felt like the mother in the supermarket who wards off a public tantrum by buying the child the coveted candy bar. I knew I was setting a bad precedent.

I fed her tiny bits of cake praying she wouldn't choke, and her face lit up with a glow as if that cake had candles. I made her drink some of the coffee sludge they provided to help it go down. None of the staff were nearby and we got away with the misdemeanor.

After dinner I wheeled Mom back to her room. Gloria bustled around smoothing out the sheets, fluffing the pillows, and filling Mom's water cup. I adored Gloria. She was my favorite staff person. Mom liked her, too. She had fantastic fingernails painted in crazy colors and designs, big bright gold jewelry, and her hair was a mélange of stiff and intricate waves that reminded me of the wigs The Supremes wore. She was a big Black woman with a large energy field that filled the small room. I averted my eyes as Gloria put fresh pull-ups on Mom. Pull-ups are really diapers but no one uses that word in Bayview. There are a lot of euphemisms in the nursing home world.

"Do you know what your mother did the other night after you left?" asked Gloria. Mom was pretending she didn't hear the question and focused on the television.

"No, I can't imagine," I said, playing straight man.

"Well, she began hollering and banging on her bed tray yelling about how she wanted to go home. She disturbed everyone on the hall."

"Really," I commented, not at all surprised. I knew it was only a matter of time. Mom was not one to go gently into any place she didn't want to go. The honeymoon period was over.

"Oh yes, really. She's not being a good patient, and her a nurse and all. I know she knows better."

My mother had not taken her eyes off the TV.

"Well, I have to go now, and I hope that doesn't happen again." I leaned over to kiss Mom goodbye. "I'm leaving now," I said again, heading for the door. "Mom, promise me you won't yell anymore."

Mom looked at me like a repentant child. "Okay, I promise," she said, and then in a very soft voice added, "unless it's absolutely necessary." She had a mischievous smile on her face, and I rolled my eyes and shook my head at Gloria. "I'll see you tomorrow. Now be good, Mom." I walked away as fast as I could so as not to hear any protests.

Out in the hallway, I had to smile. My mother had always been in control of her situation and this one was no different. Secretly, I had to give her credit. They couldn't make her do what she didn't want to do. Nobody ever could. I still hoped she would improve, but the doctors said she wouldn't. They said she would always be totally dependent and always need round-the-clock care. I didn't completely believe that was true, but things weren't looking promising.

I resolved right then to help her in her fight to have things as much her way as she possibly could. I thought she should have some control over her life. For a start, I'd get her food restrictions modified if possible. Eating is one of the most enjoyable aspects of life and I wanted her to have that bright spot in her boring day. There should be menus with choices on it in nursing homes just as there are in other large institutions like hospitals and schools. I insisted that a substitute be made available anytime my mother did not like the menu. I understood it had to meet her dietary restrictions. The staff accommodated me, and it wasn't really that hard. A cold sandwich, or some sliced turkey and vegetables, or a hearty soup with crackers and cheese spread, were not difficult to rustle up. After all, the goal was to keep her eating so she wouldn't lose weight and would receive nutrients she required. Bayview went along with my requests and Mom was happier and so were they.

CHAPTER 40.

Gloria to the Rescue

June

By the time June arrived, Mom's behavior had deteriorated and she was no different than she had been at Pleasant Gardens. She began crying and begging everyone near her to take her home. All the progress I thought we had made in making Mom happier in her new setting was short lived.

One day Gloria waylaid me in the hallway as I was on my way to visit Mom. "Well, your Mom caused quite a ruckus here last night. I almost called you, but then we calmed her down."

"What happened?"

She leaned in closer to me. "Your Mom was screaming she wanted to go home and if she couldn't she'd rather be dead!"

I listened to the rest of the story in dismay. Mom had been thrashing around in her bed and wouldn't let anyone near her. Finally, she let Gloria get her into her night gown and stopped yelling. Gloria stayed with her talking to her in a soothing voice until she was almost asleep.

"The reason I'm telling you all this is because I want you to know I'm going on vacation next week. She's gotten real attached to me and I can't predict what will happen if I'm not around. You know how they are with medication......."

I understood that without Gloria there that night, they probably would have medicated Mom, and that could continue if the problem persisted.

"I'll try to be here more. What else can I do?"

Gloria shook her head. "I don't know. I just wanted you to know what happened. I know you can't be here all the time; then you'd be a staff member."

Gloria had a point. I was there on a daily basis; I shouldn't have felt compelled to be there more. Mom was paying a lot of money to have full-time, professional people tend to all her needs, and yet, that wasn't enough. I had a sinking feeling in my stomach.

"Where are you going on your vacation?"

Gloria gave me a megawatt smile. "We're going to Disney Land. Me and the Reverend are taking our three grandchildren. I've been saving up for this trip for five years. It's the first time for us all."

I remembered Gloria telling me how much she wanted to take her grandchildren on this trip. It's tremendously expensive for anyone and especially for someone making only about $26,000 a year. I thought of my friends' kids and how many times they had been to Disney Land, most of them multiple times. The children I met in White schools regarded a trip to Disney Land as something every child did, at least once. Mom took Melanie and me to Disney Land once and it was one of the highlights of my childhood. I was painfully aware of two different Americas; one where children expected Disney Land to be part of their childhood, and one where children like Gloria's grandchildren dreamed of going there and for some, that dream never comes true. Gloria was determined to make that dream a reality for her grandchildren and it had taken her years to be able to afford it.

Aides are required to have a high school diploma plus training to become a nurse's aide. Training programs vary but most are six months long. They spend an average of two hours and twenty minutes with each resident per day, more than any other staff member. Most are paid hourly at about twelve dollars an hour. They work under the supervision of nurses or physicians. They feed, dress, groom, and bathe the residents and assist in general record keeping. Because they have the most contact with the residents, their interactions with them are critical to the mental health of their charges. They are vital staff members, and yet, are among the lowest paid workers in America.

Gloria was acutely aware of her importance in the lives of the residents. She had enormous empathy for them and worked hard at developing and maintaining relationships with them. She was a gem and always had time to talk with the residents and try to get a smile from them.

I was happy for Gloria to be able finally to take her grandchildren on the trip, but I knew my mother and I would miss her. She had become an important part of my mother's well-being, witness the night she described. Other aides were friendly, but Gloria took extra care to be with my mother and tend to her special emotional needs. Gloria was her friend.

"Thanks for telling me and I hope you have the trip of a lifetime! Mom really likes you and she'll miss you. So will I."

"Oh, now, I'll be back in a week. I'll talk to your Mom about my trip, so she'll be prepared. She can be a handful, but she's got some kind of inner strength that makes her rebel here. I call her "tiger" sometimes, and so does the rest of the staff. We understand how she feels and try to make it as good as we can for her here. After all, she's one of us, a nurse, and we respect that."

Gloria hurried off to tend to other residents. My eyes were a little moist as I watched her go. I was so thankful for Gloria, someone who shared the responsibility for Mom with me. I felt so alone the minute she walked away.

CHAPTER 41.

Unclenching Therapy

At times Mom's continuing unhappiness and intense, unrelenting desire to "go home" made my insides clench up in a ball of pain. Sometimes it happened right after an unpleasant visit with her and other times it happened at night when I couldn't fall asleep as my thoughts turned to Mom. I tried to breathe through it, taking long inhalations and then letting them out slowly, but I couldn't relax. I felt intense, unmitigated guilt, over the fact that I had not somehow brought Mom home to live with us. She was so desperate! How could I not figure out a way to accomplish it? Then I would remember a phone conversation from long ago.

I was getting a divorce from my second husband, Dan's father, and I decided I had to change my career path from teaching to something more financially rewarding so I could support myself and my young son. I decided it was not too late to go to law school. I believed I could pass the entry test and then get that coveted degree. Law was something that was appealing to me, not only as a way of increasing my income, but as an avenue to fight for the rights of people with disabilities and other disadvantaged groups. I called Mom in Florida.

"Mom, I've been thinking of going back to school and becoming a lawyer. Danny and I need a better income now that I'm getting a divorce. I could do it, if I could live with you a short time until I got myself settled. I could work in the day and go to law school at night. As soon as I could, I'd move somewhere nearby and then I'd only need you to help out on days during the week when he wasn't in school. I could get a babysitter after school to cover those hours."

It was an audacious request, I knew, but I didn't want to be in a dependent position ever again. When I went to college, women rarely went to school to have a career that was lucrative. We always thought, unrealistically, that we would be married someday and therefore could work in careers that would be rewarding and/or enjoyable to us, the opposite of what most men thought. The idea of supporting myself was not something I really had ever envisioned.

There was a long pause on the other end of the line and then Mom said, "But, Bethanie, you know we never got along."

After some more uncomfortable silence she added, "Ben and I have many friends down here and we're really busy with them. I don't think it would work out."

"Okay, Mom, I guess you're right," I said, feeling crushed. I had called her in desperation. I thought that, because her mother had done the same for her, she would understand and be willing to help me work toward a better life. But that was not something she wanted to do. Sometimes, I'd recall that conversation, and it helped me feel less guilty and my insides would unclench. The only way Mom could "go home" was to come and live with me and that was unrealistic. When I asked to live with her, she made a choice to say no. No one wants to completely disrupt their life for someone else, and yet some do.

I wound up staying in teaching and kept on getting certificates and more degrees so I would be eligible for the higher salaries available in education settings. It meant leaving the direct instruction of children and going into administrative positions. I always missed working with the children, but it was a necessary step to gaining my independence.

CHAPTER 42.

The Caregiver Support Group

July

Mom had regressed. She was no longer talking and spent her time sitting in her wheelchair making her unhappy noises and rocking back and forth. Whenever she saw me, she stopped and stared at me with recognition, but then looked away. The dips and upswings in the rollercoaster ride of my mother's condition were depressing me more than ever. I decided to talk to the nursing home social worker about it. She was there to help residents as well as their families. I asked if I could talk to her about my mother and we went into her office. As soon as I started talking, I began crying.

Theresa looked at me across her desk, tilted her head to the side causing her fruit earrings to waggle and said gently, "You know your mother is not so difficult when you're not around. She doesn't sulk and make so many of those moaning sounds when you're not here. I've gotten her to sit in on some of the activities even though she hasn't participated yet. I talk to her, and she usually responds to me as well as the rest of the staff. I'm not saying she's perfect, but she's not as bad when you're not here."

I looked at her incredulously. This was hard for me to hear. It was good news and bad news. Mom was not as bad off as I had thought and was adjusting to being there. On the other hand, my presence made her behavior worse. I felt like I had been punched in the stomach. All this time I had believed it was imperative that I visit her daily to keep her spirits up and I was having the opposite effect.

"So, my mother is playing me a little bit."

"A lot," said Theresa. "She knows you and resists you. It's taking a toll on you. She eats for other people, not just you. She makes eye contact with other people including me. She shuts her eyes tight when she doesn't want to hear what someone is saying to her. She seems to enjoy having letters read to her or looking through scrapbooks that we have here."

I felt ridiculous and angry at the same time. This was so typical of our relationship, and I had missed it.

"Why don't you try visiting every other day and give Mom more of a chance to adjust to Bayview. The visits might be able to be cut back to once every third day or so. After each visit I want you to do something that makes you happy. It could be getting an ice cream cone, or going shopping, or getting exercise."

I began following her advice. An ice cream cone is a real mood elevator and forty-five minutes at the driving range made me feel energized and ready for whatever came next. I didn't go home and nap anymore. I managed to stay awake and before I knew it, it was time for dinner and Jack was home.

I went to a few caregiver support meetings and got some interesting feedback. Theresa ran the group, and it was much smaller than I had expected. People only came for a few sessions and then stopped. I got the impression that there were a lot of people who were as upset about their parents being in a nursing home as I was, but they had adjusted or maybe their parents didn't present the same problems as Mom did. Most of them said their parents had adjusted although it was hard at first because they continually cried and begged to go home. The group consensus was that my mother probably behaved differently when I wasn't there because she was able to be who she was without embarrassment or sadness or anger in front of the people and staff who never knew her before. It was a revelation. Of course! I reminded her of her former life. This was her new life and she had begun to accept it, but I was still focused on her getting better and getting out.

I went to several sessions and the discussions were so upsetting I cried every time. I was embarrassed, but I couldn't control myself. The group thought it was normal that I should be depressed and urged me to take time to do other things and stop feeling guilty. With their help, I came to the realization that I didn't want to do enjoyable things because I felt guilty about having a good time when she was having such a miserable time. When I pointed out that other residents seemed so much more accepting of their fate, Theresa said many of them had been there longer. The length of time in a nursing home is a factor to be considered, she went on. The adjustment period can take a year. In October it would be a full year that Mom had lived in nursing homes, first Pleasant Gardens, now Bayview.

I didn't feel good about this explanation because it made me think a lot of these people had given up hope of getting better and that's why they adjusted. They had no other choice. They were not necessarily so well adjusted to their new life as they were resigned to it. I still thought that shouldn't be the case. If one must live in a nursing home, why couldn't it be a more joyful place and not so institutional? Efforts to deinstitutionalize have been the trend for years in other institutional settings. People with disabilities are being placed in more home-like situations such as group homes, and smaller living areas where the residence is broken up into pods with a communal living area, kitchen, and activity room within the large building. The more progressive nursing homes incorporate pets, plants, and more steady interaction with smaller groups of people. They try to provide a homier existence. They seek to reverse the forced dependency by letting residents have as much input as possible into their lifestyle.

I wish my Mom could have been in a place like that, but I didn't know of any place like that nearby. I think it would have made it easier for her to adjust to such a life changing event.

CHAPTER 43.

Some Younger Residents

Not everyone at Bayview was old, I discovered. It is a county-run facility and sometimes people end up there because there is nowhere else for them to go. Jorge arrived one Saturday with an entourage of relatives speaking Spanish to him and to the staff, sometimes all of them at once. Jorge, a big, heavy, fourteen-year-old hemiplegic also diagnosed with hemophilia, was fairly stuffed into his wheelchair. His relatives buzzed around him like bees circling a large flower and couldn't do enough for him. They brought him food that he preferred like pizza and chicken nuggets. Different relatives of all ages kept coming and going throughout the day. I couldn't imagine what he was doing there amid all the elderly people and I would have felt sorry for him except for the fact that, unlike his fellow residents, he had company all the time. They constantly talked to him, fed him, and laughed with him. It was like a big party in the dining room or the sitting area whenever they were around. Not surprisingly, Jorge never appeared downcast and was obviously delighted with the attention and the lively company. I asked one of the aides why such a young person was there. She explained that there was no place else to put him at the moment, but he was due to be placed somewhere else soon.

He was gone after a few days. I hoped there would be young people wherever he ended up. Unless he needed continuous medical care, there was a good chance he would be in a public school or possibly a special education school. Since 1975 when the Education for All Handicapped Children Act was passed, every effort has been made to include even students with severe disabilities who require many accommodations to be able to go to school with non-disabled students. Jorge and his boisterous, animated, caring family created a brief pocket of life and joy in Bayview. What a lucky boy to have such a vast support system, so unlike most of the other people there.

I discovered another young person in Bayview on one of my walks around the floor, a young man who looked to be in his twenties, lying on his back, eyes closed, hooked up to several tubes and monitors. He was in a private room, a rarity. As I stood there, a familiar looking man came walking down the hall and stopped to greet me. It was Cliff, my electrician, who had done work for me for many years. He was always a garrulous and friendly guy. He owned his own company and was very successful. I sometimes ran into him and his wife at charity events where he supported various community organizations.

"Hi, Cliff," I said. "What brings you here?"

The smile on his face evaporated. He looked at me gravely. "I'm here to visit my son. That's him," he said pointing at the young man who looked so peaceful. "We went on a ski trip to Colorado last year and he crashed into a tree. He's been in a coma ever since."

I told him how sorry I was to hear that. He continued telling me the story as though he was glad to have someone to listen to his sad story.

"I thought he was going to die, but he lived and has been in this condition ever since. They say his brain waves are very minimal at this point, but I come and talk to him and pray for him to wake up. There is no other place that will accommodate him near me, so he's here, and since he's close by, I can come and see him frequently. Linda never comes. She can't bear it anymore. She prays for him, but she can't handle seeing him like this."

I told him again how sorry I was and that I hoped his son would awaken soon. The boy was his only child, and he was being groomed to take over the business when the accident occurred. How awful for that family. There is so little one can say in these situations.

CHAPTER 44.

Confronting Jack

July

Jack and I went out to dinner with another couple, a nice refreshing change of pace. I'd been avoiding socializing. Unfortunately, when they asked about Mom, I got teary. I guess that ruined the mood. I was not much fun to be with, but I didn't care enough to fake it and act happy. When we got home, I told Jack I still felt guilty that Mom was living in a nursing home. He knew exactly where I was going and headed me off at the pass.

"We don't have the right setup for your mother here. You know that. Doctors have told you it's not a feasible idea considering the continuous care she requires."

"I know, but I can't stop feeling guilty. Other families manage to care for their relatives in their homes."

"Would you really want your mother to live with us even if it could be done? You've never gotten along with her. You used to say she was like Kryptonite and, when she was near you, she sapped the strength out of you, remember?"

It was true, I did make that comparison. When she was on her way up to visit from Florida each spring, I used to joke that the nearer her car got, the weaker I felt. The truth is I really did dread her visits because I knew that the moment she set foot in the house, I would feel like I did as a child — unloved and a person of little worth. She didn't really say anything critical, but she didn't praise me either. No matter what I had accomplished, or how I looked, or what I made for dinner, or what activities I engaged in, or how my career had advanced, it was as though she had no interest in any of it. Compliments were not in her vocabulary.

During her visits she expected me to spend each day doing things to entertain her and I did. We went out to restaurants, movies, shopping, art shows; every day I planned something we could do together. When Dan was little, our day often involved him, but when he was older, he was not interested in doing so many things with Grandma. I included her in activities with my friends. They thought she was terrific and if they had a party, they insisted on my bringing her along. She had plenty of compliments for them and told me what she liked about each one. It got to the point where she began suggesting that we get together with them each visit. She seemed more interested in being with them than with me.

The other thing I hated about her visits was the open-ended departure date she insisted on. No matter how I tried to pin her down about a definite date when she would be leaving to visit her friends in north Jersey and then Melanie; she laughed it off and just stayed. Sometimes for weeks. It's hard to throw your mother out of your house, but her presence wore on Jack and me. We needed our privacy back. Jack was not eager to have it invaded again.

I had been told several times by doctors that my home was not a place that could provide the level of care and medical supervision that Mom needed. Emergency situations, especially another stroke, could not be managed quickly enough, by a family member or hired caregiver who did not have medical training. They told me some of her regression could be due to mini strokes she was experiencing, causing the increasing level of debilitation.

Despite all of that information, I would have felt better if Jack had at least said that if it were possible, he would do it. I understood the impact on our relationship would have been immense and probably detrimental, but I would have felt better if he had said he was willing to try it. But he knew it wouldn't work and wasn't going to say he supported the idea when he didn't. I know I wouldn't have liked the intrusion into our lives either, but part of me just wanted to hear him say it would be okay with him if there was any way we could do it. I would have probably backed off the minute he agreed to it.

"You know I've always gotten the impression that your mother doesn't like you. You barely rate in her hierarchy of people she likes to be with and goes out of her way to do so. I'm sorry to say this, but I've observed her with you for years and I think there is something that keeps her from being a devoted, loving mother. I don't know what it is. Maybe *you* do. Maybe you remind her too much of Leo."

I listened to Jack and knew there was truth in his words and I should accept it. I know our life would have been vastly different if we really had made that kind of change. We had the freedom to do what we wanted to do on our own schedule. I didn't want to quit my job and I probably would have had to. I guess I felt ambivalent about actually having my mother live with us; I wanted to see her happy living somewhere other than a nursing home, but the only somewhere I knew of was with me. I know my entire life would have been in a state of upheaval if she had moved in with us. Jack loved me and that was what I needed. He is the sustenance I need to keep going in the face of difficulties. I had to let go of the fantasy of having Mom live with us for many reasons.

I dropped the conversation for good.

CHAPTER 45

A Fact of Life Here: Death

July

I went to deliver some things to Mom early in the morning since I had an appointment that day. I was just about to enter her room and say hello quickly when I saw my mother, lying on her bed naked while an aide gave her a sponge bath. The curtain was not drawn. Anyone walking by could have seen her there. She looked like a corpse, except her eyes were open. I was horrified. What a total disregard for privacy and dignity. I reported the incident to the nurse in charge and she apologized. The incident made me feel, once again, that I had placed my mother in an institution where people were not treated like human beings with feelings, pride, and the capacity for being embarrassed. I hurried off to my appointment without seeing my mother.

I began to notice that some residents were not around anymore; people I was used to seeing at meals or in the hallways, gone. I never asked about them and preferred to think they'd left of their own accord and were still alive somewhere, but I knew that it was inevitable that many of the residents would die there, and my mother might be one of them. It's one of the hard truths about nursing homes. We had been shielded from this harsh reality, my mother and I, but one day it was unavoidable. Two days previously, her roommate had had a stroke, one of many she'd had over the years. The curtain was drawn between the two beds, and the daughter explained that her mother was now on hospice. She said it was just a matter of time. The woman's family members began coming much more frequently; somber, quiet people with pale drawn faces. There was no way my mother could not be aware that something had happened. Even during such a traumatic time in the life of a resident, there was a lack of privacy. The roommate involuntarily becomes a bystander as the life in the next bed winds down.

The daughter and I knew each other in a peripheral way and would exchange greetings but nothing more until this turn of events. I didn't want to intrude on her privacy, but now, I felt it would be insensitive not to talk to her if she wished. We met in the in the hallway as she was getting ready to leave. She told me her mother had been in Bayview for two years. She said she knew this day would arrive and it had been a long tough journey. I shared with her how upset I'd been about my mother and that I couldn't imagine living like this for two years. The daughter was calm and spoke very softly. She was a thin, wisp of a person, with a sad weary smile. Everything about her was plain and muted: her brown hair cut in a short straight style, her non-descript clothes in tones of gray or brown, her half smile. She worked in an office. She always came alone. She said at first it was hard, but as her mother declined she came to the realization that there was no other option. Her mother accepted her life at Bayview after a year. Her mother's condition kept deteriorating and even she knew this was her life for the remainder of her days. I asked the daughter if she felt guilty sometimes. She said yes but explained that there comes a time of acceptance, and you do whatever you can and that's all you can do. We both ended up crying and hugging out there in the hallway. We ignored the staff who passed by us and they discreetly looked away.

Two days later the bed was empty. My mother and I never spoke about it. Once again, I thought of my mother's favorite aphorism, some things are better left unsaid.

CHAPTER 46.

Getting My Marriage
Back on Track

July

Jack and I had been married twenty-five years. We'd had our share of problems, but we'd come through them. Financial setbacks, stepchildren, juggling our careers and home responsibilities, the disappointment of not having a child together, all of it surmountable. Our marriage worked on the principal of balance. If I was having a tough time, he'd make me laugh and put everything in perspective, my personal court jester. If he was feeling down, I would show my undying support for him and assure him that whatever came our way, we would get through it together. The experience of having my mother in a nursing home and all the guilt I felt about it put a tremendous strain on our relationship. I finally came to the realization that my mother would be in a nursing home for the foreseeable future and that it was the place where she would get the kind of care she needed. It was far from a perfect arrangement, but my role was to provide a counterbalance to that life by being there for her. I told myself that was all I could do; I was doing the best I could. Merwin's words often reverberated in my head, "No one could do more." I let go of my fantasies of having her come home.

In Genesis, the Bible tells us "A man shall leave his father and mother and shall cleave unto his wife: and they shall be one flesh." It's a phrase I interpret as being true for the wife as well; leave your parents and cleave unto your husband. I am not religious, but I appreciate the wisdom I sometimes find in the Bible. I was comforted by that command. Our relationship had to come first. I couldn't continue to allow my mother's misfortune to overshadow our great fortune in having found each other and getting to spend the rest of our lives together. My mother would be gone one day, but I would have years and years to spend with Jack, my wonderful husband and best friend, the man who loves me more than anyone ever has. I would never desert my mother, but I had to make my marriage my priority.

CHAPTER 47.

Please See Me, Know Me

July

I stopped in around 4:00 PM just to change things up and keep the staff on their toes. Relatives of residents who have been in nursing homes for a lengthy period of time advise that you should visit at different times, so the staff is not prepared for your visit. They weren't prepared.

Mom was sitting up in bed watching TV. The bed tray was pulled around in front of her and sitting on it was an untouched bowl of soup and a small dish of fruit salad. I asked one of the aides if it was a snack or what. She said it was part of Mom's lunch since she hadn't eaten much during that meal. My Mom cannot eat drippy things with a spoon by herself. There's too much spillage due to her difficulty keeping a liquid substance on the spoon all the way from the bowl to her mouth. Why would anyone put soup and fruit salad on her bed tray and think that she would be able to eat it? I made a mental note to complain to the nurse in charge and then I started feeding her. Bayview was better, but still had the problems of inadequate staffing.

Mom looked up at me brightly and said, "I can't believe you always come."

"Of course, I do. Why are you surprised?"

"I just didn't know you cared that much."

I let that sink in and gave her a donut I'd bought for her.

"Oh, that's nice," she said picking up the donut. She took little bites and seemed to savor each one. It was a French cruller, soft but not crumbly like cake or cookies, so I knew it wouldn't choke her.

Her words stung me. How could she think I didn't "care that much" when I'd been there almost daily? She said a similar thing once when I was helping another resident get comfortable in his bed chair by adjusting his feet on the footrest when he asked me to. It wasn't hard to do, and I didn't think it was a big deal. The poor man was one of those who must stay on a slanted bed almost at a forty-five degree angle all day because he can't be in a wheelchair. I tried to help out when I could because the limited staff could never meet all the needs that existed among those severely disabled people. After adjusting his feet, I went back over to Mom sitting nearby, observing my small act of kindness, and she said, "I didn't know you were so kindhearted." I looked at her incredulously and responded, "Why do you think I went into special education? Because I'm hard hearted? Why do you think I've devoted myself to Family Services fund raising and volunteer activities? Because I don't care about people?"

It was at that moment that I realized my mother's view of me had nothing to do with anything I did outside of our sphere. To her, I had been a problem and a person who sometimes fought with her and exchanged harsh words. It wouldn't have mattered if I was Mother Teresa — in her mind I was still Bethanie, the difficult daughter. No matter what I did or how I changed when I got older, her perception of me was frozen in time. Instead of getting angry and feeling misunderstood, I decided to just continue to show her through my actions how much I really did care. I decided I'd keep trying to undo the years of damage that had led her to the conclusion that I was not a caring, kind person. I wanted her to know me and see me as others did before it was too late.

I drove home, my vision blurred by tears. Why did it have to be this way between us? Throughout our relationship, no matter how much I wanted some praise, some acknowledgement from her that I had done some good things as well as bad, I never received it. I began remembering some of the things I had done where her praise would have been normal for any parent but was absent. When I got a lead role in the high school senior play, I never heard her say she was proud of me. When I spent my early years in education as a speech therapist, then a learning consultant, and later a professor of special education, I don't recall her ever saying a word that would indicate she was proud of me. When I got my master's degree and then my doctorate, she seemed uninterested. At one point, she asked me, "what do you need a doctorate for?" I do remember her telling me once that I was a good mother. When I started writing a column for the local newspaper she demonstrated little interest. I did these things for myself, true, but I would have liked hearing her say she was proud of my accomplishments.

I wanted to say before it was too late, "Mom, please see me, your daughter, whose life has been one of accomplishment along with failures, regrets, and mistakes," but I decided I could only convey these thoughts through my actions.

CHAPTER 48.

A Visit from a Grandchild

July

was feeding Mom her lunch when my twenty-nine-year-old son, Dan, my only child, entered the dining room. He's six feet five inches tall, broad shouldered, well-built and his fair skin and shaved head make him look even larger and more imposing than he already is. He doesn't walk so much as glide and, whenever he enters a room, it's like watching an ocean liner majestically part the waters as everyone looks up and moves aside. He was a bouncer in one of his early part time jobs and had no trouble with any patrons, even though he's never been an aggressive person or much of a fighter. His size and calm demeanor combine to allow him to handle challenging situations quietly and effectively. It's always been his style since he was a child. He went to Tulane University, dropped out after sophomore year, and decided to stick around and learn the restaurant business in a town known world-wide for its delectable, indigenous food, and huge restaurant scene. He was an assistant manager by this time and happy with his career choice. He had a few rare days of vacation time from the upscale New Orleans restaurant where he worked and decided to come home for a brief visit. Dan hadn't seen his grandmother since before her stroke.

"Look who's here," I said, hoping she'd remember him.

"Hi Grandma. It's me, Dan." He leaned over to kiss her on the cheek. She smiled broadly but didn't speak.

Dan had spent a lot of time with her when he was young. She came to visit us every year in New Jersey or when we went to Florida to visit her for a week at Christmas time. Mom always lavished affection on him. As often happens with grandparents, they have better, more satisfying relationships with their grandchildren than their own children because they are free from parental responsibilities and can just enjoy the child. She, who had so many rules and consequences, would admonish me when I imposed any on Dan. I never hit him, because I remembered the handprints and all the crying and because spanking and all forms of physical punishment were frowned upon by the time I became a mother. Instead I used the latest child psychology methods. Mom didn't see the need to impose any rules or restrictions on her adorable, charming, little grandson. Much to her delight, he used to entertain her friends by singing "The Sun Will Come Out Tomorrow," this beautiful blond boy who really could sing and continued to do so as he got older and sang the lead in an amateur rock band. Everything he did was "wonderful," and he was "so bright and such a good child." Where did all this praise come from in the mother I knew, so stingy with her compliments to me?

I lifted the spoon to her mouth, and she ate what was on it, but her eyes never left Dan. She accepted the food automatically, like a robot. Dan talked to her about his job, his girlfriend, his deaf cat, and the sweltering heat of a New Orleans summer. Mom was mesmerized by him. I don't know if she was listening to him or just absorbing his presence. I reminded them of funny incidents that occurred when she was taking care of him while Jack and I went on trips, and we all laughed. Family lore, always a touchstone.

"Remember when you and a friend took the kayak out on the bay and Grandma called the police to find you?"

"Yeah, Mom, I'll never forget the Coast Guard coming alongside us. We thought we had done something criminal."

We both laughed and Mom gave us a slight smile. No doubt she remembered that incident when she thought she had lost her grandson.

"I'm sure you don't remember when I used to feed you like this," I said to Dan as I fed Mom another spoonful of something. "You were a good eater as a baby. Your favorite food was baby food peaches in those little jars. Remember?"

"I do," he said, "because I made you buy them for me all the way up to first grade. My palate has expanded since then."

When lunch was over, I wheeled her back to her room and the aide took over. She had eaten well and was ready for a little nap. Dan leaned over and gave her a kiss goodbye. She was beaming but still did not speak to him. She hadn't been speaking much for the last few months.

As we walked down the hall he was silent. Then he said, "Grandma isn't doing too well, is she."

"No, she's not. She's declined every month. It's not good."

"Can she talk?"

"She can, but she doesn't choose to most of the time."

"You're really patient with her; the way you're taking care of her."

"Let that be a lesson to you," I said in a mock serious tone, "I expect the same from you when I'm old and infirm." We both laughed and then, after a pause, as though considering this carefully, he said, "If I can, I will." He gave me his serious, intense look, the one I knew was honest and sincere. He's not one to promise things he may not be able to fulfill. He'll probably be too busy or far away or both. I don't really expect it of him either. I think I'd rather just die than be so com-pletely dependent on anyone; children, nurses, or aides. That's what I say now, but who knows. It depends on the quality of life I have. I hope my fate is not my mother's even though I know that heredity plays a huge role in your health. I inherited bunions and migraines from her; please let it not also be strokes.

Two days later, I drove him to the airport. "I had a good time, Mom. Thanks for everything," he said as we hugged. "I'm glad I saw Grandma," he added before disappearing into the terminal. I think we were both thinking it might be the last time he'd see her.

I'm glad he has a memory of a grandmother who loved him and thought he was perfect. That's what grandparents eventually should become — beautiful memories from someone's childhood. I never had that. As a grandmother, Mom surpassed anything I expected from her. She adored Dan and he knew it. I'm grateful to her for that.

CHAPTER 49.

Friends Caring for
Their Aging Parents

July

I had two friends I was close to who were also caring for aging parents. Sometimes I talked to them about what was going on in my situation with my mother, but I didn't want to burden them. They were sympathetic and supportive, but what could they do besides listen? They both liked my mother very much and went to visit her. Their parents were not as incapacitated as Mom; yet. They'd each seen me break down a couple of times talking about it, and they had tried to comfort me. Afterwards, I didn't feel better — I felt pathetic. That's not what I wanted to do when I was with them. The best thing they could do for me was go places and do things with me and not talk about it, so I steered away from that conversation. I needed a respite from my preoccupation with Mom.

Some lucky people have elderly parents who are healthy and independent, but many have parents who are increasingly dependent on them. Illness, mental and/or physical, slowly whittles away at their parents and the problems get bigger. The adult children, many of whom just became emancipated from child rearing responsibilities as their own children became independent adults, have new responsibilities involving their parents. Talk among this group revolves around doctors, living arrangements, and taking over their parents' affairs. There are websites that provide caregivers with emotional support, resources, and suggestions for overseeing all the aspects of being a caregiver, but one size does not fit all. Each family is different in their relationships with each other and in their financial resources.

The one common outcome I've noticed, is that when it's all over, the children are glad they put in the time and effort to make their parents' lives easier, despite the impact on their own lives. Recently I spoke to an unmarried man about forty years old who moved in with his mother and took care of her for two years while she wasted away from cancer. When he described how difficult it was and how much of his life it consumed and how he did things for her he never imagined himself doing, I commented on how hard that time must have been. His immediate response was he'd never give up those years with her.

I was starting to feel that way myself.

CHAPTER 50.

Winding Down

August

I t was hard for me to believe that Mom had been living in a nursing home for almost a year. The time had gone by slowly, yet when I thought back to September when all this started, it was like it had just happened. Two years is the statistic most often given as the length of the average nursing home stay. I assume the people in the statistics died because if you're in a nursing home that long, you're probably in very bad shape. Some sarcastic residents used to say they believed the only way they were leaving was in a box. When I looked ahead, I finally had to acknowledge that Mom might never leave.

Bayview was definitely an improvement over the first nursing home. They never gave up trying to get her involved in activities and reinstituting various therapies when the time seemed right, and when Medicare would allow it. She had a few surges of progress in motor skills during the first two months there, but then began to decline. She was still in her wheelchair and was never able to make it move on her own. She still needed assistance with all daily living tasks. She could eat with her left hand, but slowly and not reliably. She had become much less verbal but still responded to people who talked to her by nodding her head to show assent or dissent.

Having Mom in Bayview and seeing her calm down and accept her life more, allowed me to adjust, too. I began to enjoy my life again, my family, friends, work, activities, even though the realization of what Mom's life had become was a black cloud hovering over me most of the time. I was still despondent to think that this was her life.

Bayview had adjusted to Mom, too, and that had made her more content with her surroundings. They let her stay in her room in the afternoons if she wanted to and used to let her stay up at night with the light on to watch TV, but that had become unnecessary — she went to sleep soon after dinner. Her life had become increasingly a life of slumber. I guess that is not so unusual for someone in their mid-eighties.

I no longer took her out on excursions anymore. The last time was when I decided to take her shopping for new bras. We got in the car, and I explained we were going to Boscov's to get some new bras and maybe other clothes she needed. After five minutes in the car she began to have a meltdown, rocking and moaning. I pulled the car over to the side of the road. "What's wrong?" I asked her. "I want to go home. I don't feel good." I took her back to Bayview. Shortly after that attempted shopping outing, Mom stopped wearing bras because the staff thought she would be more comfortable without them, and she didn't really need the support. I guess they were right. Who needs to wear a bra if you spend most of your time sitting in a wheelchair or lying in bed? Despite her complete lack of interest in leaving Bayview for outings, I put up a temporary ramp in the garage over the three steps leading into my kitchen in case something changed, and I could get her there for a visit.

Mom had adjusted to being in a nursing home, at least outwardly, up until this month. Then something changed. When I visited she looked at me with recognition but responded to nothing I said. I imagined her glare was one of reproach. Why did you put me here? Why are you still coming around? After a few minutes of this penetrating stare, she would turn away from me and look at anyone else passing by or in the room. It was like being shunned. Why do I continue to visit, I asked myself? Because if I don't, she may not receive the care she needs was my answer. I couldn't take that chance; she couldn't feed herself at all at this point. So, I endured her cold accusing stare even though it felt like being stabbed in my eyes with long pointy icicles.

Lately she had begun engaging in strange stereotypic behaviors. She combed her hair with an invisible comb. She fondled a tissue box and turned it over and over in her hands. The doctor said this was not abnormal at her stage of deterioration. He said there was nothing to do about it. It was just some behavior that she engaged in almost unconsciously.

When I spoke to her, her eyes hardened and bored into me like lasers. She was angry, and I didn't blame her. She knew where she was and who I was. I was the person who put her there and never took her home. She was much less physically capable than in previous months — it was hard for her to stand even with support, she couldn't assist her aides when they dressed her or bathed her, she was limp. Who wouldn't be angry?

Although the social worker and people in the caregiver support group advised me to visit less, I kept coming just about every other day. To do less felt like desertion. I was her only link with the outside world, the only human with whom she had a personal connection. Seeing her deterioration and feeling her silent rebuke was extremely hard to take.

I began having a recurring dream. I was on a big ship with Mom, and it was sinking. We had to take what we could and go up on deck. Mom wasn't in a wheelchair. She was sitting on her bed in a corner of the stateroom just staring at me refusing to get up. The ship tilted and water came sloshing into the cabin. I was looking down at her from an angle and stretching out my hand begging her to come with me. She continued to look at me in silent determination with those intense, fierce, brown eyes. She defied me and made no attempt to move from her bed. At that point, I would wake up. I never saw the end of that dream, but I knew how it ended.

By mid-August Mom was growing more detached. She still recognized me, but she stared at me when I talked or asked her questions. It was as if she'd taken a vow of silence. She still talked minimally to staff members if she needed to, but not to me. I felt she was receding more each day. I didn't feel like doing anything anymore. Maybe I was unconsciously mirroring her behavior. At one point I sat on the bed and just held her close to me. She stayed there quietly, not resisting, not responding, like a human rag doll. I thought to myself, maybe this is all I can do for her now; just let her know I'm still here for her; and she's not alone.

I didn't visit for a couple of days because I didn't think she cared. I got her arm protector pads for the wheelchair and stockinettes for her arms to protect the bruises and skin tears that appeared due to her very thin skin, a part of aging. They'd downgraded her diet by two levels because choking had become a problem again. She also had to be protected from possibly inhaling her food because she was losing the ability to eat normally. Sometimes when I fed her, she began gurgling and regurgitating dribbles of food. I would stop feeding her and alert a nurse who would check vital signs. She always concluded all was fine.

To see my mother in this state was devastating. After all the effort put in by both of us, she'd come to this. For the first time I felt hopeless. Was this inevitable? She was only eighty- five. I knew she would not improve; the question was how long would she live?

When Merwin called to say he was coming for a visit, I told him he needn't, she was so unresponsive. "I know I don't have to, but I want to. I need to for myself." He was there the next day. She didn't show any sign of recognition. She was curled up in a fetal position and that was the end of his visit. I know it killed him to see her like that, but he said, "I needed to say goodbye. She was a good sister."

In late August I began going to visit and check on her less frequently, about three times a week. She was being fed and not losing weight, so I didn't need to concern myself about that. She would drift off into sleep and then wake up abruptly, on and off the entire day. Feeding had become a contest to keep her awake long enough to eat. I spent time just waiting for her to wake up so she could eat some more. Her eye contact with me was minimal. No more accusatory staring, now she pointedly ignored me. She was more interested in other people who walked by or staff who asked her questions. She followed the movements of the people around her with her eyes and would nod sometimes in response to questions the staff asked. She seemed very content in bed and protested at being put in her wheelchair. Mom was drifting off into her own world. Watching her decline and seeing her in this condition was torture.

Even though Mom was not in pain, I believed the life she was enduring constituted suffering. She was weak and frail and lay in bed most of the time. I knew this mission was over for me. I knew I needed to get busy with life again. I took on more assignments at work and began volunteering again to help with some charities I had dropped out of. For Mom there was nothing more I could do but keep an eye on things. Sadly, all the money she so carefully saved was dribbling away. She'd have been so unhappy to know it. She bequeathed money to Dan and Melanie's two children in her will, but it looked like there would probably be very little left for them after her death. That's what happens to many Americans in nursing homes. They use up their savings and then have to go on Medicaid or rely on relatives or both. Fortunately, for Mom, both Melanie and I had resources we could tap in to if needed.

Merwin called and wanted to visit again, but I told him it wasn't necessary and described Mom's condition. This time he didn't argue with me; he'd surmised as much from his last visit. He said he prayed for me and Mom and hoped I wouldn't dwell on this. He added he understood how much I'd suffered. These were unusual words coming from Merwin, a man who rarely revealed deep feelings. Thank heavens for his presence and reassurances through the entire experience.

The jade plant I bought had continued to thrive without much care all this time, but now it was beginning to slowly die. I watered it and tried to bring it back to life, but to no avail. The plump leaves were shriveling and dropping one by one. It's a coincidence, I told myself, but it was as if without my mother's love, the plant was withering just like her.

CHAPTER 51.

Gertrude's Choice

September

M om was listless all the time. When she sat in her wheelchair, she would fall over to one side. One eye stayed half closed. They'd been feeding her puree. She ate maybe one meal a day. The rest she let dribble out of her mouth. When I arrived that evening, Lottie was just about to call me. She told me Mom had stopped eating and taking liquids. The next step could be to send her to the hospital for an IV, but she saw the family had signed a DNR and thought they would not want to prolong her life with forced feeding. The other option was to keep her comfortable and keep trying, but things didn't look good.

I couldn't speak. I broke down and began to cry.

"I feel like she hates me," I sobbed.

"She doesn't hate you. She knows you've been a devoted daughter."

"But how can we allow her to starve?" I asked.

"It's the family's choice to make, but this is often how things end. The person who is allowed to die is not in any pain. They are given appropriate drugs to make them comfortable and are cared for as far as hygiene and attention to their vital signs and any other needs that arise. Some families feel that this way is death with dignity."

"How long will my mother last?"

"It varies in different cases, but it could be a couple of days or several." Then she gave me an impulsive quick hug and walked hurriedly away.

I left the room, called Melanie, and told her it was important for her to arrive as soon as possible — Mom was dying.

I couldn't make my mother live when she didn't want to, and she had made that clear by refusing to eat. Actions speak louder than words. The spark that lit my mother's persona had been dying since she had come to the realization that most of what had been attempted to get her well wasn't working and her future was to be dependent and live in a nursing home until she died. My mother could not and would not accept that scenario. How could I force her to keep on going? How could I usurp her role in her own fate? There was a quality of life to consider when making such a grave and enduring decision, but even more importantly, there was the person's wishes. She wasn't in pain, and she was conscious of her surroundings for brief periods, but for my mother that was not life — it was a living death.

She was such a vital person, so full of life and interests. Mom lived a very full life, counting even the troubled times, because she persevered and made the most of life. She had lived life on her terms and even now, at the very end, she was in control. She could have eaten or drank, but she chose not to. Again and again I saw that defiant look on her face when she turned away as someone tried to put food between her lips. She would close her lips tightly and turn her head to the side. I became convinced she had made the decision to end her life; taking control as she always had. This was the last thing I could do for her; let her go.

173

CHAPTER 52.

A Death Watch

September

Watching my mother die was the most heart breaking experience I have ever had. I never thought I'd be right there with her when she took her last breath, but I know that when people die at home in hospice or in a hospital, that is often the case. I was totally unprepared for the experience as I guess most people are. She began to sleep more and gradually went into a coma. Her breathing became different, first faster, and then it was slower. She was given pain medication throughout. Melanie and I were with her day and night for three days. We sat on either side of her bed, each of us holding a hand. We talked to her and put ice chips on her lips to keep them from cracking. It was torture, but we both agreed that, as my sister said when she saw Mom's condition, "this is no good." I knew it was the right action to take when Melanie said that.

The staff was so supportive and kind as they waited and watched and tended to her needs. Several of them told us how much they liked her and respected her for her unwillingness to bend to all the rules of the nursing home. They admired the feisty former nurse for her resistance to authority, even though they were the authority, and in many ways, they had bowed to her will. One by one, they stopped in to say goodbye to one of their own. It was almost midnight on the third day of our vigil when Mom took several deep breaths, one great shuddering breath, and then just stopped. Melanie and I were frozen, waiting to see if this was really the end. After several seconds, I summoned the nurse. She rushed in and checked for vital signs. "I'm sorry," she said, "your mother is gone. I'll leave you alone with her for a while." Melanie didn't move from the bedside as tears streamed down her face. Even though it was never something she would initiate, I felt a need to hug her and be hugged. I walked around the bed and wrapped her in my arms for a few minutes. There was nothing we could say.

We'd been through a lot over the past year and our relationship had probably changed, but it was too soon to tell. Over the years, from the time Melanie was little right through our adulthood, Mom expressed the wish that we would be close because she "wanted us to have each other in life." Up until now we hadn't been close, but I felt a change was coming. Mom would have been happy.

CHAPTER 53.

A Revelation

The funeral in Florida was small, just a graveside service. Merwin couldn't make it down to Florida and would attend a memorial service back in Jersey. Melanie planned to go to the memorial service up north, as well. The presiding rabbi did an excellent job of paraphrasing my sister's, my uncle's, and my words. Mom was buried next to Ben as she wished. Melanie wrote the epigraph for the headstone which reads: A joyous traveler on the highway of life! The reference to her love of driving and traveling in general is an aspect of Mom that was well known, but Melanie picked it because she saw Mom as a joyful person traveling the highway of life, not just Interstate 95. For me it summons an image of Mom taking on the road of life with an indefatigable spirit and optimism. Nothing could stop her once she got something in her mind; she was a force of nature and was never defeated until the stroke beat her down.

There were only two other people present besides Jack and me. One of Mom's closest friends, Jeanette, the one she knew from nursing school who joined the army with her where they served together in Europe and remained her friend through all the many phases of their lives, was present. Her son had brought her. She was using a walker and looked tired and gray. I remember her being such a kind person with a great sense of humor. She and Mom had their misunderstandings but had remained friends and stayed in touch intermittently over the years. She moved down to Florida around the same time as Mom and Ben did. After the service she said, "Your Mom always talked about you. She was so proud of all your accomplishments." I must have looked astonished because she continued, "Oh, yes. She used to carry around newspaper articles about your achievements and those essays you got published." It was a revelation to me, of course. How I wish she had told me how proud she was. But that was not her, for whatever reason. It was comforting to learn how she bragged about me, though I never would have thought it.

During the days that followed I cleaned out her apartment and sent Melanie things she wanted. While cleaning out her papers I came across things of mine she had saved. Some report cards, a trip journal about the trip we took across the country to Arizona that time, and the most surprising thing of all, a few index cards meant to represent pages in a story I wrote, probably the first one I ever wrote. There were my drawings and my penciled printing that told the story of *The Little Note*. I remembered the story about a musical note that came to life and jumped off the page in a music book to explore more kinds of music. I must have been taking piano lessons at the time. What struck me was that she had saved it. She must have thought it was special. Maybe she thought I was special, too, but just could never tell me.

CHAPTER 54.

The Loneliness of the
Ambivalent Daughter

September

t was a balmy day in late September. I was sitting on my patio, the one with a new path made of pavers leading up to it so that a wheelchair could traverse more easily than the previous flagstones. The Montauk daisies nodded their heads in the slight breeze. The red, purple, and white border of vinca plants was still colorful but getting a little leggy this late in the season. Chickadees were busy at the birdfeeders that emerged like green metal plants on tall stalks here and there in the lawn. A couple of squirrels chased each other around and around the oak tree in a crazy game of tag or hide-and-seek. The whole backyard was dappled with sunlight, and I relaxed in the warmth, my body free from tension and worry for the first time in a long time, and yet, I felt immense sadness. I had anticipated sharing this lovely setting with my mother where I knew she would enjoy the birds and wildlife and tell me the names of the flowers and give me advice on what to plant and how to care for it. She was an expert at cultivating all flowering plants, especially rose bushes, which I had not planted yet — I wanted her to help me pick them out. The plan was that they would have been *her* roses and we would have enjoyed their fragrance and loveliness together during frequent visits to my home.

I felt like a deflated balloon sitting there in my garden, limp, still. I had nowhere I had to go — I could sit outside and just be. I felt free. I was now officially an orphan, my new status. It was a relief not to be worrying about Mom, but at the same time I felt an emptiness, as though my body had suddenly become hollow. A cavernous hole existed inside me where all the concerns, the plans, the wishing, the hoping, the fear, the anguish, the to-do lists, the schedules, the determination, used to take up space. I never dreamed I'd miss it all, yet I did. There was a constant sense of purpose that kept me so engaged with life. I knew then that I would miss it until other things filled in the void left by her death. How I missed her! How I had wasted much of the time I could have shared with her and didn't because of a problematic history. Before the nursing home placement, I used to call her every Sunday morning to check in and share whatever was happening in my life and listen to what was going on in hers. I thought of it as an obligation; but now I would have given anything to have been able to call her and talk and talk and not hurry to get off the phone as I used to. I'll never have her in my life again, I thought, nor anyone like her, and the loneliness was overwhelming.

A small plain white butterfly was fluttering around the daisies. It flew about slowly and landed delicately within a foot of me for what seemed like an inordinately long time. I stayed still as a rock. "Mom?" I said softly.

Epilogue

I n the process of writing this book, I saw my mother with different eyes. In reviewing not only her final year, but other incidents from the past and revisiting the people who were important in her life, I came face to face with the complete and unabridged Gertrude. I could not continue to view her in a negative vein; I had to look at her and see the total person. I encountered a brave young woman who rebelled against her parents and married out of her religion, who went abroad to help wounded soldiers in a war that could have ended her life, who was a single mom to two young daughters while holding down a full time job, who introduced me to so many things that have enriched my life, who survived a heart breaking, disappointing marriage and went on to make a life with a man she grew to love and cherish. She was a loving, attentive grandmother and a loyal friend to her many friends who called her their most stubborn friend but accepted her despite that. She was a woman who fought courageously to overcome the devastating effects of the stroke before she gave up and decided to leave this world.

All the months of being with her, day after day, helping her to fight for her life and her dignity, led me to know the truth — I have always loved her just as she had always loved me. During one of our many fights, I remember saying to her "sometimes I don't think you love me." I was a young married woman at the time. I still remember her response clearly as if she were right here sighing and saying, "Oh,

Beth, you'll never know." I know now. Not everyone loves in the same way. There is no perfect love, there is only love that overrides and endures despite the relationship problems and vicissitudes of life.

Ironically, after she died, one of my friends told me that Mom had confided to her that she wasn't sure if I loved her. I was so surprised to hear this and understand suddenly that neither one of us felt loved by the other and each of us wanted to feel that. I was ambivalent in my feelings about her, and I realized that she had been ambivalent about me, too. If only we each could have understood that love is not about saying "I love you," although that's what every child wants to hear — it's about the ways you show your love.

How fortunate I was to have had this time with her, finally getting to know and appreciate her. Though she was so unhappy much of the time following her stroke, I believe she got to know me, too, and saw a side of me she had not known before. Taking care of her over the past year brought so many memories back and I saw the pattern of giving love and then withholding it that marked our relationship, on both sides.

In every writer's training, at some point they are instructed to show not tell. How much more important that is in real life! She showed me how much she loved me by caring for me in her own way my whole life. I was able to show her my love by caring for her at the end of her life. I hope her doubts were erased.

Appendices

THE RESIDENT'S BILL OF RIGHTS
The Nursing Home Reform Act established the following rights for nursing home residents:

1. The right to live in a caring environment free from abuse, mistreatment, and neglect.

2. The right to live without the fear of enduring physical restraint.

3. The right to privacy.

4. The right to receive personal care that accommodates physical, medical, emotional, and social needs.

5. The right to a social contact/interaction with fellow residents and family members.

6. The right to be treated with dignity.

7. The right to exercise self determination.

8. The right to exercise freedom of speech and communicate freely.

9. The right to participate in the creation and review of one's individualized care plan.

10. The right to be fully informed of any changes to the care plan or status of the nursing home.

11. The right to voice grievances without discrimination or reprisal.

PREVENTION OF ABUSE IN LONG TERM CARE SETTINGS
American Association of Retired Persons

Education and training for staff

Cultural issues

Interpersonal skills

Witnessing and reporting abuse

Problem solving skills

Managing difficult residential care situations

Humane salaries

Adequate staffing

Enhanced communication between staff and administration

Opportunities for upward mobility

TEN STEPS TO REFORM AND IMPROVE NURSING HOMES
National Center of Elder Abuse

1. Require more registered nurses

2. Partner with Hospitals

3. Improve infection control

4. Reduce social isolation

5. Address the funding

6. Revamp the staffing model

7. Improve oversight and reporting

8. Rethink ownership

9. Provide more care at home

10. Create smaller nursing homes

REFERENCES

American Association of Retired Persons AARP
(http://www.aarp.org)

National Center on Elder Abuse
(http://ncea.acl.gov)

Medicare
(http://www.medicare.gov)

Family Caregiver Alliance
(http://www.caregiver.org)

Politico 2020/05/26
As Residents Perish, Nursing Homes Fight
for Protection from Lawsuits.
(http://www.politico.com)

The Green House Project
(http://thegreenhouseproject.org)

Acknowledgements

First and foremost I want to thank my sister, Melanie Cutting. She stood by me and my mother during the last two years of our mother's life driving down from Canada to New Jersey on an incredibly frequent basis. Without her support, assistance, and wise advice, my time as a caregiver for our mother would have been a very different story and much more arduous and overwhelming. When I began to write this book, she read multiple versions and edited them all. She never gave up on the project, no matter how many years I worked on it. She is a trained editor and I am forever grateful for her expertise. Our mother would have been gratified to know that we, the daughters she had always wished would have a close relationship, became devoted sisters who resolved of our historical misgivings and came to understand each other better as we worked on this project together.

I could not have written this memoir without the encouragement and support of my husband, Jack, who gave me all the time and privacy I needed to work on it. He understood how important it was to me to finish this memoir and once said writing is a part of me and I need it to fill a particular space in my life. The insights he shared on the nature of my relationship with my mother gave me valuable insights and additional perspective.

My cousin Phil Fuchs and his wife Barbara encouraged me to move forward and get the book published. They were both very fond of my mother and approved of the book which showed sides of her they never knew, but they understood the book is meant to show the true natures of all the characters, including myself to the extent I could.

I want to thank my writing groups, first at the Kimmel Center in Palm Beach, Florida and later at Florida Atlantic University. They listened to chapters from this book and encouraged me to keep writing. As early readers they let me know that the tender story of mother and daughter moved them and the nursing home descriptions were illuminating and introduced them to a world most of them were unfamiliar with. Some said they thought it was an eyeopener for people who might have the same experience and would help them be better prepared for the planning and the emotions it describes.

My friends Saundra Newman, Patti Lang, and my sister's daughter-in-law, Janine Cutting, all of whom are voracious readers with an eye for what makes good writing and a well told story, read the manuscript, and offered their suggestions and encouragement. Their enthusiasm for the story gave me confidence to pursue publication.

About the Author

D r. Bethanie Gorny has worked in a variety of education positions including as a special education teacher, a learning dis-
ability consultant, a child study chairperson, director of special
education services, and a professor of special education. She holds a
master's degree in Learning Disabilities and a doctorate in Education.

Her writing has been published in
The Atlantic City Press, The Phoenix Jewish
Journal, The Florida Writer Magazine, The
Jewish Literary Journal, WildWord.com,
Jewish Fiction.net, Pleaseseeme.com, The
Sun Sentinel, McSweeney's online, and
others. Her first book *Fridays with Eva*
was published by Amazon and is avail-

able on their website. She won first place in the Royal Palm Literary
Competition for her short story memoir *The Blind Date of a Lifetime*
and received honorable mention in the *Writer's Digest Awards* in the
category of nonfiction short story.

She is retired and lives in Boynton Beach with her husband Jack.
She is active in organizations for the elderly, Holocaust survivors, and
is president of her condo association. She spends her time running
book clubs, playing golf, exercising, visiting her married children in
California and Chicago, and of course, writing.

Bethanie and Jack

Melanie and Bethanie

Mom in the nursing home

Mom and Merwin

Mom and Ben

Mom

Lt. Gertrude Fuchs